D. A. Horton is one of the great young minds in the American church. *Intensional* is theologically rich, incredibly practical, and inspiriting.

> **DR. DERWIN L. GRAY,** lead pastor at Transformation Church, author of *The High Definition Leader*

Horton has blessed Christ followers with a needed exhortation, framed in biblical language and categories. Perhaps this will give the saints pause in the world of needless jabs and barbs on social media. Chapter 7 is especially helpful with its categories and questions. Prayerfully, this book will lead to us ramping down the rhetoric and ramping up the thinking! Horton has served the body of Christ— yea, the Christ that prayed that His followers would be united.

> **KEVIN L. SMITH,** executive director of the Baptist Convention of Maryland/Delaware

D. A. Horton is the rare Christian leader whose superior intelligence and eloquence are matched and even exceeded by his exemplary Christian character. Those qualities come through in this magnificent little book grounding ethnicity in the imago dei and urging the Christian community toward ethnic conciliation. Even—and especially—for the reader who might disagree with certain aspects of Horton's treatment of this controversial topic, *Intensional* offers much food for thought. Highly recommended.

> **BRUCE RILF** ... *ican Christian*

D. A. Horton is ... of ethnic conciliation and ... d churches to perpetuate ethnic division ... th American church. D. A. is an outstanding thinker and missional practitioner, and in this book, he brings these skills to bear on this crucial topic. A worthy read.

> **ALAN HIRSCH,** author of numerous books on missional leadership, organization, and spirituality; founder of 100Movements, 5Q Collective, and Forge International

In my opinion, one of the greatest challenges facing the body of Christ in today's world is how to navigate with grace and wisdom an ever-increasing cultural divide between ethnicities within the church. In *Intensional*, D. A. Horton has given us an incredible work that will help Christians move forward with compassion, humility, and true repentance regarding those longtime ethnic tensions. This is a timely, much-needed book that I cannot recommend highly enough.

MATT CARTER, pastor of preaching at Austin Stone Community Church

When I was an assimilated soldier in the army, I only saw green— and Jesus was green, too, since that's where I thought I met him. When I transitioned out of the army and into full-time ministry, I thought Jesus didn't see our colors, just our hearts. Jesus then began to begin to chip away at me and brought me to the reality of my own heart.

Intensional is a powerfully written perspective for the reader who *chooses* to consider and engage in the conversation about ethnicity and the people of God. D. A. Horton goes into the depths of where the issues are: in the heart. This is a great resource for those who are really willing to look and engage. I'll be chewing on this for a bit; this book has been a breath of fresh air as I've been trying to figure out how to engage and implement these ideas in my ministry. I am encouraged to have had the chance to read this.

VICTOR HUGO PADILLA, The Navigators—Military

I'm so grateful for my friend D. A. Horton, who has provided redemptive language that enables us to engage across the ethnic divide in a way that glorifies God and honors our fellow image bearers. His is a needed prophetic voice for such a time as this.

BRYAN LORITTS, lead pastor at Abundant Life, author of *Insider Outsider*

In a world where things are often black and white—even in the church—it's so refreshing to hear yet another voice, a powerful one, that can add to the greats of our time, saying things others avoid, yet with love. To use D. A.'s own words, "The complexion of America is browning both socially and spiritually." As a Latino, I'm so grateful for this voice, perspective, and transparency to the church from his heart! #EnHoraBuena

RUDY RUBIO, pastor at Reformed Church LA

D. A. Horton has yet again given the church an accessible work to help Christians pursue the unification of all things and all people in Christ—and to help them make this pursuit a normal rhythm of their Christian discipleship. Readers may not agree with everything herein, but they will learn much from this gifted brother!

JARVIS J. WILLIAMS, associate professor of New Testament Interpretation, The Southern Baptist Theological Seminary

I'm thankful for the voice of my friend D. A. Horton, for such a time as this. With pastoral care and prophetic courage, he provides an honest assessment of the church's need for "ethnic conciliation." *Intensional* is as much a compass as it is a magnifying glass. It helps us better see the sins of partiality and color blindness in the church in America, and it also provides tangible ways for Christians to live out their Kingdom identity. Pick up this book, and you'll find that there's much work to do—and a reason for esperanza (hope).

ERIC RIVERA, lead pastor at The Brook

From the very beginning of this book, I sensed that this is what the church needs—honesty, hope, and direction in a fractured time here in America and abroad. Let us remember to be intentional in the midst of the tension.

OSAZE MURRAY, Bowie State campus director, The Navigators

God has lovingly but firmly compelled me to labor for "ethnic conciliation," D. A. Horton's preferred terminology, as opposed to "racial reconciliation"—"ethnic" because our construct of race is biblically unsound and practically harmful, and "conciliation" because "reconciliation" assumes we were previously living in unity. This pursuit has sometimes left me feeling like Horton, "flirting with the belief that hate [has] won." But Horton brings the esperanza (hope) of the gospel into everyday experiences. His life experiences and biblical scholarship deliver practical and eternal guidance. By the end of the book, I'd been inspired to engage more deeply, convicted enough to change, and equipped enough to move. Please, my friends, read this book and join us.

BRIAN JENNINGS, author of *Dancing in No Man's Land*

In calling readers to biblical conciliation, Horton challenges the familiar and faulty binary of racial idolization on the one hand and color blindness on the other. If taken to heart, the theological and ecclesial road map offered by Horton will do much to restore the witness and testimony of the church in the United States during this divided time.

ROBERT CHAO ROMERO, J.D., PH.D., pastor at Matthew 25 Movement, associate professor of Chicana/o Studies and Asian American Studies at UCLA

Horton's powerful voice clarifies how the gospel of Jesus Christ exposes and heals racism, hate, and cultural compromise. Horton draws us to ethnic conciliation through Christ's redemption; his call to the church resounds with unrelenting hope. Readers who long for scriptural foundations and practical expressions of ethnic conciliation in their communities will find insight here. Highly recommended.

DR. HEATH A. THOMAS, dean of the College of Theology and Ministry at Oklahoma Baptist University

INTENSIONAL

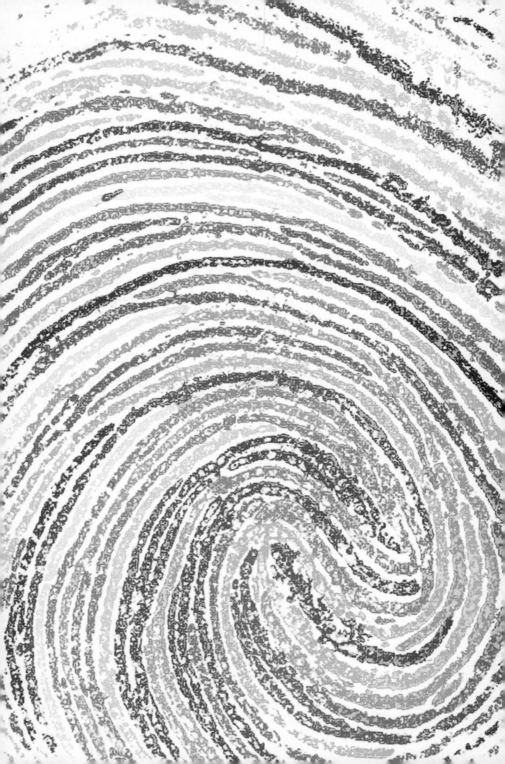

INTENSIONAL

KINGDOM ETHNICITY IN A DIVIDED WORLD

D. A. HORTON

A NavPress resource published in alliance
with Tyndale House Publishers, Inc.

NavPress is the publishing ministry of The Navigators, an international Christian organization and leader in personal spiritual development. NavPress is committed to helping people grow spiritually and enjoy lives of meaning and hope through personal and group resources that are biblically rooted, culturally relevant, and highly practical.

For more information, visit www.NavPress.com.

Intensional: Kingdom Ethnicity in a Divided World

Copyright © 2019 by D. A. Horton. All rights reserved.

A NavPress resource published in alliance with Tyndale House Publishers, Inc.

NAVPRESS and the NAVPRESS logo are registered trademarks of NavPress, The Navigators, Colorado Springs, CO. *TYNDALE* is a registered trademark of Tyndale House Publishers, Inc. Absence of ® in connection with marks of NavPress or other parties does not indicate an absence of registration of those marks.

The Team:
Don Pape, Publisher
Caitlyn Carlson, Acquisitions Editor
Elizabeth Schroll, Copy Editor
Dean H. Renninger, Designer

Published in association with the literary agency of Wolgemuth & Associates, Inc.

Cover photograph of fingerprint copyright © Andrey_Kuzmin/Shutterstock. All rights reserved.

Author photograph copyright © 2015 by Matt Engelking. All rights reserved.

For information about special discounts for bulk purchases, please contact Tyndale House Publishers at csresponse@tyndale.com, or call 1-800-323-9400.

ISBN 978-1-63146-691-5

Printed in the United States of America

25   24   23   22   21   20   19
7   6   5   4   3   2   1

para mi gente

CONTENTS

INTRODUCTION

Saturday, August 9, 2014. Police officer Darren Wilson shoots and kills Michael Brown in Ferguson, Missouri, igniting a firestorm. Long-simmering tensions boil over. And the church begins to honestly wrestle with the tension between law-enforcement officers and citizens of color, the value of African American lives, and how to respond to the anger in the hearts of Millennials and Generation Z.

As my family and I watched the nonstop coverage in the aftermath of Michael Brown's death, I reached out to a dear friend, activist and rapper Thi'sl. Thi'sl was working to gather the people in West St. Louis, Ferguson, and Florissant together for a time of expressing themselves, lamenting as a community, and hearing a message of hope.[1] I lived in Atlanta, and he asked if my wife, Elicia, and I would be willing to drive up to shepherd bleeding hearts alongside pastors in St. Louis.

When Elicia and I arrived at Friendly Temple Missionary Baptist Church in West St. Louis, we joined longtime friends and other pastors in the back room to pray before the event. Then singer Brian Owens opened with soul-stirring renditions of two of my all-time favorite songs, "People Get Ready" by Curtis Mayfield and "A Change is Gonna Come" by the legendary Sam Cooke. The room briefly filled with comradery and hope—but the optimism was short-lived. Unresolved tension would soon fill the room.

The other pastors and I sat on the stage, and Thi'sl set up a microphone at the base of the stairs for anyone who had something to say or a question to ask the pastors. Within a matter of seconds, the line ran down the middle aisle all the way to the doors of the church. When the young man who was third in line grabbed the microphone, none of us knew that his words would shift the course of the entire evening.

He gripped the mic and looked at all of us pastors. "No disrespect to any of you men," he said, "but I'm going to talk to my people." He then turned to the crowd and began to let out his anguish and pain—not only about the killing of "Mike Mike" (as the Brown family and friends of Mike Brown affectionately called him) but also about the hatred that had long held the community of Ferguson hostage.

The people hung on every word that came out of this

young man's mouth. Amid his passion-filled speech, I realized that his turned back represented the community's true feelings toward the church and its leaders.

I'm a Millennial. Many in my generation view the church as an absentee parent. The hostility, hurt, and disappointment I heard from younger Millennials and Gen Zers when they talked about the church that night was similar to what I've heard from young people who grew up without their biological father. These young people were asking, Where was the church when their cousins were killed in the streets, or when their lights were turned off, or when they had no food in the refrigerator? These urban youth grew up just trying to survive the city streets of St. Louis, and the church hadn't been there for them then. Why did they need the church now?

For the next two hours, none of the people from the community acknowledged the pastors on the stage. I listened to a community in pain: members of the Brown family, Mike Brown's lifelong barber, police officers of color. The grief and pain moved me to tears.

And so I stepped into the tension. I took the time to look into the eyes of the hundreds of people in that church, and as I did that, God spoke clarity into my heart. In the first two rows sat civil rights activists of color who had marched in the sixties. I found comfort in the gray hair on their heads and the hope that filled their eyes. They had been here before, and their legacy infused me with a profound desire to press on. Yet they were in the minority. Most of the people present were my age or younger and often rolled their eyes or shook their heads in disagreement when the older generation spoke hope-filled words from the microphone. I saw hopelessness in the eyes of my generation. Their pain was real, but their disconnection from the generation who had fought for their rights uncovered an entitlement—one that I must confess is present in my own heart. As Millennials, we are filled with zeal and want immediate change. Our hearts often grow discouraged when we do not see fruit from our short-term efforts. The irony is, in our lifetime, we have feasted on the fruit of seeds sown by the genera-tions that came before ours. We inherited privileges that they were hosed down, lynched, shot at, beat up, and jailed for. As I sat in that church, I realized that we have not had to endure half of what our elders had to.

Our entitlement clouds our judgment and often leads to a subjective understanding of justice. That day, I heard three definitions of justice among the younger generation. To some, justice meant seeking retaliation on the officer who killed Mike Brown. To others, justice was finding the officer, having him arrested, tried, and found guilty of murder. Still others believed justice was looting and rioting that would allow them to get what they felt society owed them. If Mike Brown's death was necessary for them to get ahead, then so be it. And in all of these conversations, I started flirting with the belief that hate had won.

But in that moment of despair, God reminded me that the church Jesus is building will never fall victim to the evil one. In intentional times of dialogue, fasting, fellowship, and prayer, we as believers have the opportunity to meld together, to stand alongside one another against despair and hate. As we go out to live on mission, we hold the message of hope in tension with the hopelessness around us—and as we do, we can plow the hard, fallow ground and sow seeds of righteousness.

But we must do it together. We cannot enter into the tension alone, not when the hatred around us is so strong and the hope is so weak. That night, watching the hope of the older generations in that room, I was reminded of farmers who would yoke together an older and wiser ox with one that was young, strong, and inexperienced. The older would help carry the load, but the brunt was carried by the younger—while the older ox patiently guided the young one, teaching it to plow straight.[2] The body of Christ is a multigenerational body. We need to work together—the older among us sharing guidance and wisdom with the younger, and the younger using our passion and strength to move the plow. At the end of the day, God is the one who brings the increase (1 Corinthians 3:6-9); our role is to plow, plant, and water.

HATE, HOPELESSNESS—AND HOPE

As the event ended, Elicia and I felt discouraged by the task at hand. As we headed for the door of the sanctuary, a man began walking toward us. I had noticed him earlier in the evening. He wore a beautiful body-length dashiki, and gray dreadlocks flowed from the top of his head all the way to his calves. He'd been sitting in the very front row. Every time words of hate were spewed, he was unmoved. Whenever words of love and Scripture were spoken, his eyes would become relaxed, and he would smile and gently nod his head.

He reached out his hand to take mine and asked if he could share a few words from his heart. He walked me through his participation in the civil rights movement when he was young and strong. The bright-burning hope he'd once had for the future of both the church and the American nation was now a low flickering flame. He told me that he had entered the church tonight with a prayer that God would show him that the baton that his generation had carried would not be dropped or thrown away.

That was why he had come to find me. He told me that a few responses I shared from the stage, before the young man turned his back on us, turned up the flame in his heart. He heard compassion in my voice and saw that I shared the Scripture with passion. Then he asked, "What is your ethnic heritage?"

"Mexican American, Choctaw Nation, and various European ethnicities," I told him.

He smiled. "I have always witnessed that blacks do not want to listen to whites and whites do not want to listen to blacks," he said. "But I have sensed that God desires to raise up voices of other colors that would be able to reach both sides, because those men and women can sympathize with each side without having to fit the profile of either." He told me to embrace my brown voice to breathe fresh hope into a conversation that has so often only been about black versus white.

The United States has boasted of being a white Anglo-Saxon Protestant (WASP) missions-sending powerhouse,[3] but it is looking less European and Protestant—and more multicolored—by the day. As Derwin Gray said in *The High Definition Leader*, "The face of America is no longer just black and white, like those old televisions from back in the day. America is in high definition now, filled with different colored people."[4] The complexion of America is browning both socially and spiritually, and this is not necessarily a bad thing. Brown is the color that becomes visible when every primary color is mixed together. This diversity provides space for America to be seen for what it truly is: a mission field that is ripe for the harvest—and a place where the beauty of God's Kingdom can be made more visible.

The pulse of America's new mosaic rhythm beats to the

tune of relativism, and its compositions sit comfortably at the top of the charts. The ever-confused subgenre of Christianity fights for pole position in the mainstream it once dominated. In 2017, Gallup reported that 48.5 percent of Americans identify as Protestant, which shows a drastic decline from 63 percent in 1975.[5] The term *Protestant*, as used in Gallup's report, is inclusive of subgroups such as evangelical, Jehovah's Witness, and mainline, each of whom disagree on essential, secondary, and tertiary issues in philosophy of ministry and theology. We've arrived at a time where *Christian* and *Protestant* are being reimagined, and the profile of each resembles the Global South more than the America of yesteryear.[6]

Relativism is leading an exodus of nominal Christians out of the church and into the world. Is it too late for the church in America to engage the culture so she can fulfill her mission? The mission of the church is to preach the gospel of the Kingdom, make disciples of every ethnicity, and socially engage the people in our communities, serving them as representatives of the Kingdom of God.[7] That mission remains intact despite the spiritual and social changes in America. If the church desires to live on mission and have maximum impact for God's Kingdom, it must shift its methodology but not its message. And the voices who proclaim the message must include Kingdom people, men and women, who are of African American, Asian, European, Latina/o, Middle

Eastern, and Native Indigenous nations descent to reflect the Kingdom of God as we see it in Revelation 7:9.

It's taken me thirty-five years to stop fearing and fully embrace my brown*ish* voice. I say brown*ish* because my story is not the typical Mexican American story. I'm a third-generation Mexican American who was raised in a predominately African American neighborhood in Kansas City. My music of choice was hip-hop. My favorite singer is Sam Cooke. For a period of ten years, I loathed the idea of eating Mexican cuisine and opted only for Chinese, cheeseburgers, pizza, or soul food.

Growing up, I had no desire to learn Spanish because none of my neighborhood friends were Latino.[8] I never saw myself leaving my neighborhood. Culturally,[9] my friends and I shared similar experiences, like growing up in poverty, surviving among drug dealers and gangs, and sharing with each other whatever we got legally or illegally.

I empathized with the prejudice my friends encountered. I was with them when we were confronted by law-enforcement officers, shopping-mall or grocery-store security guards, and corner-store owners. I was treated no differently, even though my skin was a few shades lighter than theirs and my hair texture was different. When we were pulled over, I was asked the same questions, and I wasn't spoken to any differently. When I surrendered my heart to the Lord at fifteen, I began being more vocal about the prejudice in our community and inside the church. But even then, most of my focus was on the African American struggle.

My complexion is light, so my darker-skinned family members would call me *güero* (fair-skinned), but I was too dark to be socially accepted as someone of European descent. I was too American to be Mexican and too Mexican to be American. Too light complexioned to be accepted as African American but a little too brown to be embraced as someone of European descent.

After I met Jesus, my ethnicity wasn't affirmed in the church for years, so I put further distance in my heart toward my own ethnic heritage. I built a wall of self-preservation, where I tried to be as ambiguous as possible with my ethnicity. I wore a short haircut that would not show my bone-straight hair and give people the opportunity to assume they knew my ethnicity.

In 2011, my dear brother Pastor Rich Perez approached me after I preached at the Legacy Conference in Chicago. He told me how much it meant to him to finally see a Latino preaching on the main stage of a conference with a sizable audience. I was taken aback. In my four years of pastoral ministry and fifteen years of public ministry, this was the first time that a Latino had affirmed my preaching ministry. This led to numerous other experiences where *mi gente* (my people) expressed their joy as my presence provided them representation. My fear began dissolving.

A few days before my thirty-fifth birthday, my family and I were walking home from a local park. As the kids ran ahead, I shared with Elicia that I've finally realized who God created me to be and how He wants me to serve His body, with a specific emphasis on our *gente* (people). I told her I was embarrassed that it took me thirty-five years to finally be comfortable with my own culture, ethnicity, and skin. I'm a mixture of heritages and hues. As I said earlier, brown is the color that becomes visible when every primary color is mixed together. I am now free to express the fact that I'm Latino and so is my voice. I have sought to become more acquainted with my Mexican American heritage so I can help raise up Latino[10] voices in the church. I'm brown*ish*, and I'm *finally* glad God made me this way.

I'm just one Latino voice in my generation contributing to the browning voice of the church. I cannot and will not be seen as *the* Latino voice. There are just too many complexities and nuances in individual Latino voices in the American Protestant church. But there is an engulfing blind spot with the Latino narrative that the American Protestant church needs to pay attention to.

The Latino population in America has changed drastically over the last fifty years, due to a confluence of economic and geopolitical trends.[11] In 1960, when the conversation on race in America was predominately about African Americans and those of European descent, six million Latinos (3.5 percent of the US population at the time) called the United States home, and most of us lived in the Southwestern region.[12] By 2014, the Latino population had escalated to 57 million (17 percent of the US population) and had spread out to more than half of the three thousand counties in the United States.[13] This explosion meant that the Latino narrative found space in the mainstream conversation, and careful attention has been given to Latino Millennials' social influence—save in one crucial area.

Latino youth are being reached successfully in the spheres of politics,[14] economics,[15] and education,[16] and yet sadly, they are not being reached in the sphere of religion.[17] Latino youth are distancing themselves from the religious convictions of the older generations at a rapid pace. This reality grieves me deeply—and yet, I also see great hope. The field is ripe for harvest. God longs to reach these young people and to use them powerfully in the Kingdom of God—to show off His power to redeem people from every nation, tribe, and tongue.

My new friend in St. Louis shared this hope with me that night. "How old are you?" he asked me. At the time, I had just turned thirty-four years old. I'm a Millennial—and an older one, at that. The experiences of my life serve as a hybrid of Gen Xers and Millennials.

When I told him this, his smile grew. "My bones are weak, and I move slow," he said. "I'm growing weaker and slower—and I stopped praying for strength years ago because I realized that in my weakness, a stronger and younger generation would rise up." But he feared that he would not be able to pass his mantle to the next generation because many of the young people did not know God or His Word. "Your generation lacks endurance because they are still young," he said. Mike Brown's death was one of our first generational tests. Would we stand on the Word of God and remain in the fight, even amid voices of hate that called us away from God?

He was excited that I was neither too young nor too old. "You can keep the strength of your youth to spur on the older ones to keep running their race. And you need to use the wisdom you've gained to pour into the ones who are younger than you." He was calling me to step up as a representative—not only of my generation and my heritage but also of the people of God.

I stood stunned by the words of affirmation that he was pouring over me like anointing oil. He put his hands on my shoulders, looked me in the eyes, and told me to open my heart to God's will for how He wants to use me to help others lead His church in America toward healing. He then prayed a prayer of blessing over me, asking God for boldness and courage in my speech, longevity in my ministry, and purity in my motives. "You represent a picture of what God wants to do in America," he said. He gave me a hug and told me that his heart was now filled with hope about what God would do among His people from different nations here in America. Elicia and I walked away from that moment in awe. And just like that, I was filled with *esperanza*.

ESPERANZA

Esperanza is the Spanish word for hope. In this work of seeking wholeness in our world of ethnic division, proclaiming the gospel of Jesus, and standing against hate and injustice, I often find myself needing to have my hope refueled. Living as the voice of a Latino who is frequently asked to address an issue that has been reduced to involve only those of African and European descent is draining. My presence on panels and stages is often questioned by my generation—and all other living generations. The fact that I'm not "African American" or "from European descent only" is confusing to some and offensive to others. Let's step into another level of tension here. Because of my skin color, I am operating out of privilege when I prophetically call out certain truths about ethnic tensions in the church: I am seen not as angry but passionate because I'm not of African descent. When others, men and women of African descent, have spoken similar truths from Scripture, they are often written off as angry and divisive. Similarly, being a male provides me with privilege that sisters in the faith do not have.

Privilege is not evil in and of itself. But we should be aware of it, and we should leverage our privilege for the benefit of those in the margins, to amplify the voices of those who are dismissed.[18]

There have been times when the plowing gets hard. I've faced slanderous attacks. Stressful seasons that lured my heart into struggles with depression. On a few occasions, I've had to fight off suicidal thoughts. Other times, my generation's silent indifference toward this work, specifically the contributions I've made, echoes in my mind. Being a carrier of hope in a context where hopelessness is dominant is exhausting. Yet God always provides me with hope when I talk with Christians from various ethnicities and generations who are doing similar work. Together, we're striving to see the hope of the gospel realized—God's people together as one multicultural, ethnic, and generational people. Although we're living in the tension of being Kingdom people of different ethnicities, we're called to be intentional in following Jesus holistically—and this includes holding in tension our unique ethnic heritages while being part of a new humanity! This work does not come without struggle, but neither does it come without esperanza.

In my moments of struggle, I turn to a hymn that captures this truth. "Canto de Esperanza (Song of Hope)" by Alvin L. Schutmaat[19] reminds me I'm one part of the body of Christ, which has been commissioned by God to bring light and hope to people in every land and of every ethnicity.

Our God is for justice. And He is the one who fills His people with love. He has called His people to bring bright light and hope to every land and people group. The tension we hold as a Kingdom people is the hopelessness of our mission field in one hand—and esperanza in the other. That's why this book is called *Intensional*: because we, God's people, must *intentionally* step *in* to the middle of the *tension—all* of us—if we're going to bring esperanza to the world.

Even amid such a daunting task as healing our ethnic tensions, we are a hope-filled people who are called to pray, sing, work, and remain faithful in sharing the hope of Jesus with the hopeless. The gospel's power is put on display when our local churches show our world what a brochure of heaven looks like. God has called us to pray and work for peace. We can live as hope-filled people who have a response to both hatred and racism. The church has both the answer and the cure to racism: the esperanza of the gospel!

CHAPTER I

WHAT IS ETHNIC CONCILIATION?

Our Call as the People of God

Racial reconciliation. This is a term we're used to hearing—but we rarely see positive results from discussions surrounding it. The words *racial reconciliation* usually trigger greater chasms of division rather than healing, repentance, and togetherness.

I'm going to state a hard truth: God's people, representing so many different ethnic backgrounds, seem just as divided as the world around us. Because of this, I have serious issues with how the American church has engaged in the work of racial reconciliation.

Yes, I believe in the full power of the gospel, which, when put into in action, produces evidence that Jesus' redemptive work on the cross is for people from every ethnicity, gender, and social class. I believe that all those who embrace Him as Lord are made part of the one new humanity He has created and is building.

But my hesitation comes down to the terms *racial* and *reconciliation*.

First, *racial* indicates that there is more than one race, which I see directly contradicting God's Word. And *reconciliation* implies we're trying to get back to what we once had—as if at one point, the various ethnicities within the United States were at a point of conciliation. To me, both terms are misleading, and operating without the fuller perspective means we're dedicating effort, resources, and time to a work that is not supported in Scripture or even a historical fact. If we're focused on the wrong things, the healing we seek will never be accomplished! That's why I believe that we in the American church should reframe the conversation around our efforts toward *ethnic conciliation*.

Ethnic conciliation is accomplished when we affirm (not ignore or idolize) the ethnic heritage of every human being and seek to remove animosity, distrust, and hostility from our interpersonal relationships. I believe that the only people qualified to take up the holistic work of ethnic conciliation are those who follow Jesus—because we are the only ones who have experienced both conciliation and reconciliation (2 Corinthians 5:17-20;

Ephesians 2:11-22). Jesus' finished work has not only reconciled us to God but has also brought us—from all different ethnicities—into one family! In Jesus alone, the nations have conciliation.

Jesus has sent His followers on a global mission to make this reality visible. The church has been equipped by God with His Word and the Holy Spirit to embody ethnic conciliation as a method of both evangelism and discipleship. When the watching world sees believers from every nation, tribe, and tongue working through the tensions of life together, nonbelievers will witness a beautiful example of ethnic conciliation.

However, what has happened for hundreds of years inside the American church is the opposite of Jesus' mission. We have refused to tear down human-made walls of segregation that have divided us from one another. Because of our stubborn unrepentance, the world has walked all over our witness.

It's time for us to reestablish a credible witness on behalf of our risen Lord. Let's step back from our status quo approach of reluctantly engaging in arguments regarding "issues of race" inside the church. Just as my wife and I need to sit down and actively listen to each other list contributions and solutions to our unresolved issues, the family of God must do the same in our divisions. We must engage with a fresh perspective that reflects Jesus' rule over the ethnic tensions present inside

His own house. And we can begin by digesting the terms *ethnic* and *conciliation*.

ETHNICITY, NOT RACE

According to the Bible, the *imago dei*—image of God—is equally given to every human being in the entire human race. I believe life begins at conception, so from the beginning of every physical life that God forms in the womb (Psalm 139:13), through the time a child is born, lives, and dies, that person bears God's image. Because I am whole life as opposed to pro-life—which is often reduced to advocacy for children inside the womb while socially neglecting them thereafter—I want you to know that every person, for the entirety of their life, is privileged to bear the image of God. When people ignore the imago dei, the result is social atrocities: not only abortion but also chattel slavery, Jim Crow laws, hate crimes, and much more.

Imago dei provides every human being with God-given dignity and distinction from every other kind of creation God made. Even after the fall of man, every human being has inherited sin equally. This was passed from Adam to our entire human race, not to one or a few select people groups (Romans 5:12). The human race traces back to one common set of parents, Adam and Eve.[1]

Acts 17:26 says, "He made from one man every nation of mankind to live on all the face of the earth, having determined allotted periods and the boundaries of their dwelling place." This one man is Adam, who heads the family tree of every ethnicity on the planet. What's important to understand here is that Paul was proclaiming this truth to a group of Greeks, who believed they were superior to all other ethnic people groups! Paul debunked any belief that one ethnicity is superior to another, especially when it comes to political and military conquests.[2]

In Malachi 2:10, the prophet of God says, "Have we not all one Father? Has not one God created us?" Malachi makes a distinction based not on race but on relationship to God. God is the creator of every human being; we all bear His image. Yet God is Father only to those He has adopted into His family. This is reinforced in 1 Peter 2:9-10; Peter speaks to Christians as God's "chosen race," "royal priesthood," "holy nation," and "people for [God's] own possession." Once again, our race is not what separates us—whether we are God's own possession is what sets us apart. If we follow Christ, we are to share God's story with those who know Him only as Creator and not as Father. This is the Good News of the esperanza we proclaim: We can each be reconciled to God.

In Scripture, the first divisions between humans come not from different races but from rebellion and separation from God. At the time of the tower of Babel (Genesis 11:1-9), all people on earth shared one language, and they used this shared language to attempt to elevate themselves above God. God brought judgment on them, confusing them by creating various languages, which would prevent humans from organizing global rebellion.

We see throughout the rest of Scripture that people are often described not in terms of racial categories as we use today but rather by ethnicity, language, or geographic proximity. As Dr. Jarvis Williams notes,

> The category of race has a broader use in the Bible than in modern terminology. One important distinction is that the biblical category of race was not constructed with pseudoscience for the purpose of establishing a racial hierarchy. Racial categories were employed apart from any consideration of biological inferiority rooted in whiteness or blackness. In fact, Genesis 11:6 in the Septuagint identifies humanity as one *genos* (race/kind/class/group). The Greek term *ethnos* (nation, Gentile) overlaps with *genos*. Both terms function as racial categories.[3]

When we look at Acts 2, we see God the Holy Spirit beginning a new and unique work in the lives of Jesus' followers, providing them with the ability to speak in languages they did not know. In this passage, people groups are identified by languages connected to their geographic dwelling:

> They were amazed and astonished, saying,
> "Are not all these who are speaking Galileans?
> And how is it that we hear, each of us in his
> own native language? Parthians and Medes
> and Elamites and residents of Mesopotamia,
> Judea and Cappadocia, Pontus and Asia,
> Phrygia and Pamphylia, Egypt and the parts of
> Libya belonging to Cyrene, and visitors from
> Rome, both Jews and proselytes, Cretans and
> Arabians—we hear them telling in our own
> tongues the mighty works of God."
>
> ACTS 2:7-11

The Holy Spirit's work at Pentecost was a foretaste of the gospel being proclaimed in languages and places beyond the geographic limits of Jesus' earthly ministry. The Holy Spirit empowered believers to make Jesus known globally and locally. The gospel's power is made visible when human beings from various ethnicities hear the gospel clearly communicated in their known language and are given opportunities to embrace Jesus as their Savior.

The Bible proves that there is one human race and that within this one race is a beautiful array of different ethnicities. The racial categories we often use today in America are human-made social constructions slanted toward partiality and manifested in superiority and inferiority complexes. In *Coloniality of Power, Eurocentrism, and Latin America*, Anibal Quijano boldly declares that the Spanish creation of racial categories was mere code language between the conquerors and those they conquered. At its inception, racial categories were a way to declare who was superior and who was inferior. Quijano says, "The idea of race, in its modern meaning, does not have a known history before the colonization of America" and "it was constructed to refer to the supposed differential biological structures between those groups [conquerors and conquered]."[4] He also argues that history shows "race as a category was applied for the first time to the Indians, not to blacks. In this way, race appears much earlier than color in the history of the social classification of the global population."[5]

One of the strongest arguments for the systemic racial caste system we have in the United States is evidenced by the color-coded language we use. In his book *Working toward Whiteness: How America's Immigrants Became White*, David R. Roediger traces how immigrants from Europe exchanged their ethnic identity for the created term *white* to secure employment, housing, and other social benefits. The idea behind this term was to create an American identity. Today in America, it's nearly impossible to speak clearly on the issues of ethnicity without having to use the socially embraced terms *white* and *black*.[6] These terms were not normally used prior to colonization.[7]

In Spain, starting in the sixteenth century, the *casta* system created systemic segregation between those with pure Spanish bloodlines and all others.[8] A royal Spanish decree in 1563 declared that the lower classes of society—which included the indigenous natives, African slaves, and those with mixed blood—could only live in approved *barrios*. (Needless to say, these barrios were comfortably placed away from those who lived in the higher tiers of the *casta*.) This system also prevented those with mixed blood from upward mobility, not only in society but also in the church.[9]

Prior to the Reformation, in 1512, Spain passed the Laws of Burgos, which provided a framework for protecting their indigenous labor and ensuring their Christianization. These laws were rarely enforced, and Dominicans Antonio de Montesinos and Bartolomé de las Casas mobilized to fight for the stated rights of the indigenous peoples who were now slaves that were treated worse than animals.[10] Between 1550 and 1551, Bartolomé de la Casas debated the known Spanish scholar Juan Ginés de Sepúlveda about the horrible treatment of the indigenous image bearers. Sepúlveda's arguments were rooted in Aristotle's doctrine of natural slavery, which said, "one part of mankind is set aside by nature to be slaves in the service of masters born for a life of virtue free of manual labor."[11]

We must understand our history if we want to understand the world we inherited. Before American Protestants charge racialized language and segregation to the Roman Catholic institution alone, we need to note a sobering truth: Much of the same systemic segregation was repeated by Protestants during the colonization of what we know as the United States of America. In American church history, the social construction of race was built by the Europeans who migrated to the new world, looking for cash and converts. In the Americas, people of color have been marginalized not only in society but also the church for nearly five hundred years. Jesus once told us that we are "the salt of the earth," the taste of God for the people around us (Matthew 5:13)— but because of this systemic sin, our saltiness has lost its flavor. Losing flavor is one reason our witness is being trampled on by the feet of the world.

This socially constructed idea of race that is normal in America today doesn't find its beginnings in Scripture. In fact, Paul rebuked this foolishness in Acts 17. The church must work to not only renounce this social construct but also tear it down, because it does not reflect

Kingdom ethics or human flourishing. For far too long, God's people have normalized the sin of partiality, the false belief of different races, and the practice of segregation. We must learn to stop using color-coded language and replace it with new language that expresses the reality of imago dei in every human being. We must also affirm the richness of different ethnicities and keep ourselves from either idolizing or ignoring ethnicity all together.

CONCILIATION, NOT RECONCILIATION

Conciliation takes place when conflicting parties overcome their animosity, distrust, and hostility to operate as one united group. When I speak about ethnic conciliation, I'm often asked, "Why do away with the term *reconciliation* when it's a gospel term?" But the term *reconciliation* actually furthers my case for *conciliation*. Before the Fall, the entire human race (in Adam and his wife) were in a state of conciliation with God. There was no animosity, distrust, or hostility. In the Fall, sin separated the entire human race from God. During our separation, because of our sin, animosity, distrust, and hostility came between our entire race and God. Through the redemptive work of Jesus, every human who embraces Jesus as their Savior is reconciled to God. But reconciliation cannot take place without conciliation—and the reality of our history means that conciliation has never taken place in the United States of America, let alone in American churches en masse.

Navajo speaker and writer Mark Charles has communicated regularly about the doctrine of discovery, which addresses how the founding documents of the United States of America used language that placed the imago dei only on landowning men of European descent. He says that while we often look to "We hold these truths to be self-evident that all men are created equal" in the Declaration of Independence as proof that the founders valued equality, thirty lines below, the indigenous people of Turtle Island are identified as "merciless Indian savages."[12] Other historic American documents strip the imago dei from African slaves.[13] The Constitution had to be amended to provide rights to women and people of color; if women and people of color had been considered equal from the beginning of our nation, there would be no need for constitutional amendments for women and people of ethnic heritage outside of Europe.

The perspective of American (and white) supremacy permeated the church in profound and troubling ways. Professor Donald Scott said that Second Great Awakening Protestant preachers like Lyman Beecher and Charles Finney told Americans that America was the site of the millennial reign of Christ, so Christians were to assume it was their destiny to usher in the Millennium by providentially expanding from sea to shining sea.[14]

Diplomats, journalists, soldiers, evangelical activists, abolitionists, and pacifists leveraged such language to frame Mexico and the Roman Catholic church as enemies to American Republicanism.[15] The resulting conquest took more than half of Mexico's land—including precious oil in Texas and California and gold in California that would be discovered later—and quashed the rights of Mexican families who owned it. In the aftermath, the Mexican American citizens of the newly formed United States were not given the same rights as its citizens of European descent, as "Mexicans of color returned to a racial order where they had few civil rights."[16] Similar to Adam renaming Eve, Mexicans living in the United States had their names sound more "American." My great-grandfather Aurelio Conchola was renamed "Joe Canchola" by the US government on entering the United States. And as we know, this is only one example of the attempt to diminish and control other ethnicities within the United States.

The term *white supremacy* is commonly understood as the belief that the "white race" is superior to all other races and that "white people" should have control over people from all other ethnicities. Often, when this term is tossed into a conversation, it causes an explosion of emotions. But if we as the people of God desire to show what conciliation looks like, then we must be willing to first recognize the realities of the world around us. Records from our nation's history—from the founding documents through our current era—show that men of European descent have always held power and therefore provide us all with the freedom to name white supremacy.

This is where the pastor in me wants to speak tenderly. In America, we are encouraged to think individualistically our entire lives. In my personal experience, when I speak on white supremacy, my brothers and sisters of European descent feel the need to exonerate themselves from the collective reality of white supremacy. At the same time, generally speaking, people of color, who often think communally, can go to the extreme and say that every white person is a white supremacist.

Neither of these extremes represents my motive for naming white supremacy. My goal is not to indict every person of European descent as a white supremacist, and neither is it to place them in a position of blame for this construction of power in our nation's history. No one should feel guilty for their ethnicity. God has created each of us to be who we are. This includes those of European descent, some of whom have approached me to apologize for being "white."

Instead, my goal here is to call us to recognize the power systems in place, both in society and the church, that work against conciliation.[17] This power structure was the reason Bishop Richard Allen planted the historic Mother Bethel AME Church in Philadelphia.[18]

This power structure is also the reason why, at least in conservative, evangelical spaces, there is a scramble to diversify conference lineups, student enrollment, and church-leadership positions.

The proper response for Jesus followers of color is not to do what has been done to us and create spaces with power structures that exclude our white brothers and sisters. Neither is the proper response to continue acting as if this power structure doesn't exist. This power structure can and should be destroyed, so that unity among God's people, who are diverse culturally, economically, ethnically, generationally, and even politically, can become a visible reality. Our goal in accomplishing this is not to achieve a Marxist utopia but rather to create a straighter path leading toward the conciliation of God's people. In doing this, we can regain our saltiness and begin to flavor our communities so they will taste and see that our Lord is good (Psalm 34:8).

TOWARD OUR REALITY

Animosity, distrust, and hostility among believers from the various ethnicities have always existed in American history—and in American church history. If we desire to pursue true healing between ethnicities, then our focus as the church in America should be to remove animosity, distrust, and hostility en masse. I'm not talking about ridding society of such ills—that is not possible. But it *is* possible within the family of God—among churches made up of Holy Spirit–indwelling believers! When this happens, legitimate ethnic conciliation will become a present reality. And I truly believe that the American church stands at the threshold of becoming the first generation to actively present ethnic conciliation to the American landscape.

Right now, though, we do not reflect what Christ's work has accomplished on our behalf. Positionally, ethnic conciliation is our reality. Revelation 5:9 and 7:9-10 provide a snapshot of the multiethnic, multilingual, and multigenerational citizens who dwell in the City of God. Jesus' sacrifice applies to every imaginable ethnicity, gender, and social class and brings each of us who follow him into the family of God (Galatians 3:26-28). Christ's finished work obliterated the walls of division that separated Jews and Gentiles as well as males and females and brings us together as a new humanity, a unique spiritual ethnicity (Ephesians 2:11-22). But the American church's present reality couldn't be any further from this truth.

Power structures in the American church have built walls that divide God's people from each other: ethnic segregation, classism, sexism, and theological tribalism. If we desire to pursue ethnic conciliation and bring our positional reality into a practical existence, we must pursue three practices: (1) American church and parachurch leadership in current power structures must acknowledge the lack of Kingdom representation in their hierarchy; (2) leadership must confess and repent if the sin of partiality is present in the culture of the executive-level leadership; and (3) we all must work with diligence and in long-lasting, two-way partnerships with competent and qualified people of different ethnicities to produce fruits of repentance (2 Corinthians 7:9-11). If we do these things, we will properly address the tensions of our day while bringing forth a clearer preview of the coming Kingdom.

CHAPTER 2

OUR REDEMPTIVE ETHIC

The Basis of Reconciliation

The Bible is like a telenovela on Netflix—it's one complex story with one plot, covered in four seasons, progressively revealed through sixty-six episodes. The Bible is God's story, and the main character of God's story is not the reader—it is Jesus Christ. Before we can dig deeper into *how* we as the church can offer healing and hope to ourselves and a world filled with racism and hatred, we must examine *why* we have this hope. We find that hope in God's redemptive plan, as revealed through Scripture.[1]

SEASON ONE: CREATION (GENESIS 1-2)

In this season one of God's story, we witness God, the uncaused first cause, use His genius and power to create all things from nothing. He establishes a framework of organization to contain all that He created, fleshing out all the intricacies of His creation to order it perfectly. And as the crowning act of creation, He forms the human race from the dust of the earth.

Genesis 1:26-28 says,

> Then God said, "Let us make man in our image, after our likeness. And let them have dominion over the fish of the sea and over the birds of the heavens and over the livestock and over all the earth and over every creeping thing that creeps on the earth."
>
> So God created man in his own image,
> in the image of God he created him;
> male and female he created them.
>
> And God blessed them. And God said to them, "Be fruitful and multiply and fill the earth and subdue it, and have dominion over the fish of the sea and over the birds of the heavens and over every living thing that moves on the earth."

This passage of Scripture introduces three keys to human flourishing:

1. **The image of God.** Every human being has been created in the imago dei, the image of God. This means that we all bear, in a limited way, characteristics of God's image: qualities such as morality, personality, rationality, and spirituality that make us distinct from the rest of God's creation. Acknowledging that every person has been created in God's image is the most basic affirmation we can make about others.[2] All people, of every ethnicity, gender, and social class, have the dignity of an image bearer and are therefore due equal respect.

2. **Cultural mandate to rule over and care for creation.** God gave humanity a cultural mandate[3] to rule over His earthly creation.[4] All humans should do excellent work in administrating, cultivating, and stewarding the planet and its resources. God desires for each of us to collectively glorify and worship Him as we work, to create beautiful things, and to follow His cultural mandate with joy.

3. **Healthy family structures.** God provided humanity with the family structure. God's design for the family includes leadership and complementary

and distinct roles for the husband and wife. Men and women have been created to help each other while living in a rhythm of oneness, fulfilling the work God gave in the cultural mandate. God desires for us, through the active intimacy of husbands and wives, to create more worshipers of God who will use their God-given creativity to steward creation and help humanity flourish.

Season one ends with man and wife living in right relationship with God and each other, working together with oneness to fulfill the calling God gave them. This is the only point in human history when God and humanity had no animosity, distrust, or hostility. Conciliation was the reality of life, God's original design for creation. Soon, peace would be disrupted and lost.

SEASON TWO: THE FALL (GENESIS 3)

In season two, things take a turn for the worse as we read of the evil one's successful deception of Eve:

> Now the serpent was more crafty than any other beast of the field that the LORD God had made.
> He said to the woman, "Did God actually say, 'You shall not eat of any tree in the garden'?"
> GENESIS 3:1

Satan's tactics in the Garden of Eden are the same ones he uses today—sowing seeds of doubt in the minds of God's image bearers. His goal is to convince human beings that our Giver of Life isn't truthful when He speaks and doesn't have our greatest good in mind. When Satan is able to do this, God's image bearer begins questioning God's words and motives.

In Genesis, Eve responded to Satan with God's command from Genesis 2:17—but she added to God's command, saying that they were not to *touch* the fruit of the tree of knowledge. This was a misstep on her part. Since God's commands and words are pure, Eve didn't need to add her words to what God said. Her reworking of God's words provided Satan with an opportunity to sow seeds of doubting God's goodness. The evil one capitalized on her response: "You will not surely die. For God knows that when you eat of it your eyes will be opened, and you will be like God, knowing good and evil" (Genesis 3:4-5). This was another assault on God's character—in essence, Satan was saying that if God were truly good, He would tell her everything He knew rather than holding something back.

Eve then saw the tree and decided that it was good for food. She wanted this hidden wisdom. So she took the fruit and ate it—and immediately afterward, she gave some to her husband, Adam, who was with her. Scripture does not tell us why Adam was passive in this moment or why he didn't interject when the evil one was speaking to his wife. What we do know is that his passivity and his failure to protect his helpmate caused his heart to follow her into sin. Adam was not deceived by the evil one—he deliberately disobeyed God.

Romans 5:12 says, "Therefore, just as sin came into the world through one man, and death through sin, and so death spread to all men because all sinned." Adam was the human race's representative. When he spiritually died in the Garden of Eden, so did Eve—and every image bearer born since was born dead in sin (Genesis 8:21; Psalm 51:5; Ephesians 2:3). Because of this first spiritual death, every part of every human (body, emotions, mind, and will) has been infected with the disease of sin.

Sin is breaking the commandments God has put in place as a framework to guide us toward human flourishing. Sin has been described as missing God's mark of perfection—as though we were shooting arrows at a target and never hitting the bulls-eye.[5] Since God is perfect and holy, He rightfully demands that His image bearers live nothing less than perfectly holy lives to be in relationship with Him. Up until the moment of the Fall in the Garden, Adam and Eve had lived perfectly. Adam's decision to disobey God is when he first missed the mark of perfection.

Adam's sin and the guilty verdict it brought about was imputed onto the entire human race.[6] *Imputed* is a financial term that describes taking something that belongs to someone and crediting it to another person's account.[7] Because of Adam, every human being is born with the guilt of sin. As we read in Romans 5:12, sin passed from Adam onto every human being produced by him and Eve. Sin is humanity's inheritance.

The consequences for imputed and inherited sin are profound: We are all, regardless of ethnicity, gender, and social status, separated from our holy Creator; we are addicted to committing personal sins; and we face both physical and spiritual death. Simply put, every human heart now moves away from human flourishing and toward selfish autonomy—self-rule and an unwillingness to be held accountable for our actions—and idolatry, which means placing ourselves or created things before God.

After sin entered the world, the perfect life that once was in the Garden of Eden was over. The need for redemption was center stage.

SEASON THREE: REDEMPTION
(GENESIS 3:15—REVELATION 20)

Season two of God's story ended with humanity in darkness. Yet season three opens with a passage of hope: the first prophecy in Scripture of a hero who would defeat the evil one, death, and sin. Season three of God's story is the lengthiest because the work of redemption is complex. The Bible shows us how God progressively and beautifully prepared the world for the entrance of His hero.

In Genesis 12:1-5, we meet Abram and Sarai, who were childless. When Abram was seventy-five, God promised him three things: a family lineage with numerous descendants, a Promised Land for his family, and a global blessing tracing back to his lineage. In Genesis 15–17, God changed Abram's name to Abraham and made a covenant with him. Twenty-five years after believing God's promise, Abraham held his son Isaac in his arms—and the story of God's covenanted people began.

In Exodus, God raised up Moses, who would serve as a mediator between God and His people. The message Moses was called to preach was simple: God heard the cries of His people, and He was now liberating them and moving them into the land He promised to Abraham. God performed miracles through Moses and his brother Aaron to establish that they were indeed sent by God, so God's people would believe the message. In Exodus 19:3-6, God declared that Israel was His chosen covenanted people, called to serve as an illustration of His Kingdom. God would provide holistic flourishing if they obeyed His commands (Deuteronomy 28:1-14); if they did not, they would experience the consequences of their sin (Deuteronomy 28:15-68). And before Moses' death, God hinted that this was just the beginning. Israel was to watch for another prophet, one even greater than Moses (Deuteronomy 18:15-22). The hero was coming.

But Israel consistently failed in their call to act as people set apart for God. Their options were between worshiping idols and walking in submission to the only true and living God. They even rejected God as their king, asking instead for a human ruler. God gave His chosen people what they wanted—and that is how we meet King David (1 Samuel 8:4-9).

In 2 Samuel 7:1-17, God told David that He would "establish the throne of his kingdom forever" (verse 13). Through David, both a house for God and a kingly throne in Israel would become an everlasting reality. The people of Israel thought God was speaking of an earthly king. But God was pointing toward the heaven-sent hero.

In the book of Isaiah, God declared that Israel had failed in their mission to be a light for the world (assigned in Isaiah 49). They had continued to pursue idols and disobey God. But then God further explained His promise: He would raise up a servant who would perfectly fulfill His commandments. This servant's sufferings would satisfy God's wrath completely, and salvation would be made available on a global scale. God's servant would provide the cure for humanity's disease of sin and complete restoration from every curse.

In the Gospels, God revealed the hero and main character of His story: Jesus Christ. Matthew and Luke connected Jesus' familial lineage back to David, Abraham, and Adam, showing how He fulfilled God's continued promise. Mark introduced the prophetic forerunner to Jesus, John the Baptist. The book of John speaks of the preexistence of Jesus before His arrival in human flesh, showing that Jesus is eternally God and equal with God. John's robust introduction culminates with a profession: Jesus, who is the Word, took upon Himself human flesh and invaded the world we live in (John 1:9-18). This is what we call the Incarnation: Jesus added full humanity to His full deity—He was fully both and less of neither.

The Incarnation took place through a miraculous conception: God the Holy Spirit, without the use of intercourse, caused Mary to become pregnant. This miraculous conception has a few major implications. First, it allowed Jesus to be born without both the imputed guilt and inherited sin of Adam. Second, it provided an heir to the everlasting throne God had covenanted with David. This solves the dilemma we read of in Jeremiah 22:24-30, where God declared that the descendants of King Jehoiakim would not sit on the throne of David ever again, literally cutting off a human line to the Davidic throne. Through this miraculous conception, Jesus was able to be the fulfillment of God's covenant with David.

Jesus Himself made direct claims about being the hero in God's story. In John 5, 8, and 10, the religious leaders of His day threatened to kill Him because He claimed to be equal with God. But Jesus didn't just claim deity; He demonstrated it—and He did that most powerfully by fulfilling God's redemptive plan.

Paul's words in 1 Corinthians 15:3-8 give us a beautiful summary of the redemption that has come through Jesus:

> For I delivered to you as of first importance
> what I also received: that Christ died for our
> sins in accordance with the Scriptures, that he
> was buried, that he was raised on the third day
> in accordance with the Scriptures, and that
> he appeared to Cephas, then to the twelve.
> Then he appeared to more than five hundred
> brothers at one time, most of whom are still
> alive, though some have fallen asleep. Then he
> appeared to James, then to all the apostles. Last
> of all, as to one untimely born, he appeared
> also to me.

Because of our inherited sin, we were all born condemned—and Jesus volunteered to die in our place. His death was literal, and His burial showed the finality of His incarnational work. But as Paul declared in

1 Corinthians, Jesus rose again! The resurrection of Jesus Christ is the foundational bedrock of the Christian faith. Jesus lived a perfect life, making Him a perfect, unblemished sacrifice, who shed literal blood—the only form of currency that God would accept as payment for sin (Hebrews 9:22). If Jesus weren't sinless, He would have never been able to rise from the grave. Because Jesus' sacrifice covers our sin, His resurrection promises that we, too, will be raised to eternal life after our death. And His resurrection also points toward our future hope: Jesus will reverse the curse of sin, and He will make all things new.

When Paul called Jesus "Christ," the Hebrew word for Messiah, he was communicating the full weight of the spiritual and social understanding of the term. Israel had been looking for a political savior, and they missed Jesus because He was doing the work of spiritual redemption among them. But Jesus also initiated social redemption in His Kingdom. In our day, many people in the church want to proclaim Jesus only as a spiritual Savior, as if He gave no social commands that we are commissioned to live. But He is progressively making things new—not only in our souls but also in our relationships and in the world He created—and Jesus has chosen to use those He saved to show the world His ability to redeem and restore!

SEASON FOUR: THE RESTORATION (REVELATION 21-22)

The final season of God's story shows us what life in His Kingdom will look like. God will live in a city called new Jerusalem, and people from every nation, tribe, and tongue who embrace Jesus as their Savior will live with Him. The struggle with evil and sin will finally be over. God and His people will never be separated again. We will live in perfect obedience to His commands and enjoy life under His rule, and flourishing will be the only way of life we know.

While we live as part of God's Kingdom on earth, we must share the full story of God—not just the first three seasons. Our message must include the fact that Jesus is restoring creation holistically. As Jesus promised us in Revelation 21:5, "Behold, I am making all things new."

And we are part of that new work of God. Our marching orders are to proclaim that Jesus has guaranteed to make all things new. Classism, racism, segregation, and sexism will not be part of society in God's Kingdom. Never again will families be separated by borders and deportation. Never will children be trafficked and sold. Poverty will never claim another life, because in the City of God, death has died.

If the gospel we preach does not include this truth, we're reducing God's story. If we're not putting feet to the faith we proclaim, we're misrepresenting Him. We have been commissioned to preach the whole story of God, and diligently working to see equity, justice, and righteousness lead human flourishing serves as a visible witness of the esperanza we're marching toward.

THE MISSION OF GOD

Knowing the story of God helps us to understand the mission of God: All of creation will give glory to their creator. God sent Jesus to do all the work necessary to redeem a people for Himself. God also sent the Holy Spirit to live inside every believer, giving them the power to stop their former way of living and to walk in obedience to God. And this same Holy Spirit empowers us to tell others the whole story of God.

Before Jesus ascended back to the Father, He sent His followers to proclaim the whole story of God on a global mission to make disciples of people from every ethnic background, gender, language, and social class. The church we belong to today lives out God's mission when it serves the world as a preview of the coming Kingdom.

And that brings us back to this complex and difficult conversation about the divisions among us. God has called us to both proclaim His whole gospel message and demonstrate what Kingdom life in the City of God looks like. For centuries, one of the greatest stumbling blocks to the church's witness in the United States of America has been the ethnic—or as some say, racial—divide in the church. God has been calling His church in America to deal with its thorn in the flesh, which has been causing infection for ages. And we must answer. In this moment of redemptive history, let ours be the generation to no longer only talk about what confession, forgiveness, and repentance look like but to bear fruits of repentance. When we do this, we'll show the world the power of God, displayed through the healing relationships of those who are in Christ Jesus. Jesus desires to use *us* as a preview of His future work of making all things new. If we want to participate in Jesus' work, ethnic conciliation is our best and next move.

CHAPTER 3

OTRA VEZ

What Does Ethnic Conciliation Look Like?

Our redemption as the people of God—our story as first the conciled ones,[1] in relationship with Him, who then fell out of relationship through sin, and who were then *re*conciled—gives us the road map to healing our ethnic tensions. We can provide a Kingdom preview of ethnic conciliation because we live this high calling of reconciliation as the people of God.

But while this is our positional reality—this is what God has equipped us for in reconciling us to Himself— we don't live in this reality well as a church. Ethnic conciliation will become evident within the church only when the members of the body of Christ stop withholding the compassion of Christ from one another. The areas of compassion God is calling the American church to focus on are our character, our communication, and our communities. If the people of God begin showing each other the compassion of God in these three areas, we'll see ethnic conciliation bear fruit in our midst. The question, then, is: *How are we to show compassion?*

COMPASSION IN OUR CHARACTER

If we as Christians seek to exhibit the compassion of Christ, we should seek to remove our animosity toward each other. While we may not think we're actively living in animosity, we are exhibiting it when we avoid meaningful engagement with other Christians who are different from us and when we create microcommunities that purposefully exclude others. There's nothing wrong with befriending believers who share common personal interests, but when circles become exclusive and perpetuate othering, they have mutated into a clique.

Jesus calls us to live differently, to go beyond our comfortable cliques and into active repudiation of animosity in the body of Christ. We see His heart on this topic brought to life in one of His stories.

The Parable of the Good Samaritan

To test Jesus, a lawyer asked what he must do to inherit eternal life. Jesus asked the lawyer how he interpreted the law, and the lawyer responded by saying the law was summed up by love: loving God holistically and loving your neighbor as yourself. Jesus told him that his answer was correct and that he should do what the law says to live (Luke 10:25-28).

But this answer was not good enough for the lawyer. In Luke 10:29, he asked a follow-up question: "Who is my neighbor?" Jesus responded with a parable. He starts his story with the victimization of a man whose ethnicity is withheld (Luke 10:30). Thieves beat and robbed the man, leaving him for dead.

As he lay on the side of the road, two men passed by: a priest and a Levite. Both men saw the victim but chose to avoid him and his need for help. This behavior should not catch us by surprise—in our day, we regularly see people merely record crimes in progress on their camera phones, refusing to intervene even when people are being horrifically injured.

But then Jesus introduces a new character in verse 33, and He begins by identifying him by his ethnicity.[2] This man was a Samaritan.

We may miss the full weight of Jesus' words in our culture. When this parable was initially told, Jews and Samaritans hated each other. The Jews saw the Samaritans as a compromising group of half-breeds because the Samaritans had intermarried with the Assyrians, who had destroyed the northern kingdom of Israel.[3] In fact, the Jews tried to destroy Jesus' reputation by spreading rumors that He was a Samaritan and demon-possessed (John 8:48). The Samaritans hated the Jews as well, and in Nehemiah 4, we read of their refusal to integrate with the Jews in Jerusalem during the rebuilding of the walls. They eventually chose to build their own temple, remaining segregated socially and spiritually. We can vividly see that the Jews and Samaritans were socially segregated in Jesus' day through the Samaritan woman's puzzled response to Jesus, a Jew, talking to her in public (John 4:9).

The reality of the culture made Jesus' choice of hero in the parable a striking one: The hero was not Jewish but a Samaritan, and he was a hero not because of his ethnicity, but because he saw the victim and acted with compassion!

The Practice of God's Son

Jesus saw people, had compassion, and acted on that compassion. Matthew 9:35-38 provides us with a word picture of Jesus traveling to various cities, "proclaiming the gospel of the kingdom and healing every disease and every affliction." At this point in His ministry, Jesus had a large following. Matthew 9:36 says, "When he saw the crowds, he had compassion for them, because they were harassed and helpless, like sheep without a shepherd." The way Jesus "saw" the crowds is written in Greek to communicate that everywhere He moved,

His compassion was with Him, like the very clothes He wore.[4] Every step He took was a step with compassion toward the people in His proximity.

Jesus' compassion did not allow Him to simply tell His followers that "the gospel" is the answer while neglecting to meet their felt needs. In fact, what's amazing is that Jesus still fed the hungry, healed the sick, and cast demons out of people He sovereignly knew would never embrace Him as Messiah, Savior, and Lord. He didn't stop proclaiming the gospel of the Kingdom to them and giving them tangible expressions of God's love. Jesus acted with the ultimate balance of compassion and knowledge.

The Prescription for God's Saints

Since God's people are not omniscient, we do not know who will embrace Jesus as Savior and who will not. Yet, in light of the example that Jesus has given us to express compassion liberally, we have no excuse to withhold it from anyone. When we withhold compassion from any image bearer, not only are we out of step with the gospel but we are also contradicting the very practice of our own Savior. For this, we must repent.

We must walk in the fruits of repentance by no longer avoiding people of different ethnicities, political views, social classes, religious affiliations, or sexual orientations. Neither must we refuse to engage in the work of evangelism among sinners from every imaginable background.

In our interpersonal relationships within the church, we must practice Romans 15:7: "Therefore welcome one another as Christ has welcomed you, for the glory of God." When we refuse to welcome, embrace, or fellowship with a believer from a different ethnicity, we are failing to represent our Savior. Ephesians 4:32 says, "Be kind and compassionate to one another, forgiving each other, just as in Christ God forgave you" (NIV). All our offenses against God have been completely wiped away through the shed blood of Jesus. Because of that, we must rid ourselves of passive-aggressive behaviors that allow us to keep angst, bitterness, and hurt tucked away in our hearts. We must learn to approach each other with hearts of love and communicate in real time when offenses and sins occur. Relationships are risky, but the reward of a deeper, more meaningful relationship far outweighs the fear and risk.

God has not left us clueless. If someone has committed a minor offense against us, we have the choice to either overlook the offense by covering it with love (Proverbs 10:12) or bring it directly to the attention of the person who offended us—after we have examined our heart for sin toward the offender (Matthew 7:5). If someone has committed a personal sin against us, we must use the process Jesus outlined in Matthew 18:15. It is best to sit down with the person, open the Bible, and read Matthew 18:15 with the person who committed the sin, biblically identifying their offense. And when any of us are approached by a fellow Jesus follower about our sinful offenses, we should humble ourselves by acknowledging our sin and confessing it. When we do this, we're to receive forgiveness from the one we sinned against, which leads us to praise God. Our relationship now has more depth for expressing God's love and truth. Now that the issue has been resolved, the fruits of repentance can become visible in our relationship.

If the brother or sister does not acknowledge their sin, then the remaining steps are to be followed with church leadership involved. The goal for this process is restoration of the sinning Christian, not to publicly humiliate them. According to Galatians 6:1, restoration is evident when the brokenness their sin has caused was mended while they were shepherded toward spiritual health. Again, this is specifically for personal sins committed between believers.[5]

COMPASSION IN OUR COMMUNICATION

It is often said that actions speak louder than words. When you live in a community that lacks ethnic diversity, distrust among different people groups becomes normal and is revealed in communication. This empowers a culture to spew distrust not only in private conversations but also on social-media platforms.

If we want to do the work of ethnic conciliation, we must intentionally display the compassion of Christ in our communication. Too often, we're tempted to profile an entire group of people based on bad interactions with a few—and our speech can become careless. We communicate and create relational distrust when we say things like "you know how they are," "that's why you can't trust them," and "they'll turn their back on you to support their own." But it's hard to express distrust for people groups who are different from you when you are living in meaningful relationships within a diverse community.

The Parable of the Good Samaritan

The parable of the Good Samaritan can speak to this reality as well. A Samaritan traveling from Jerusalem to Jericho would have likely been the recipient of ethnic slurs.[6] Remember how when the Jews called Jesus a Samaritan, it was an attempt to degrade Him? That would be like someone calling me a *wetback* because of my Mexican American heritage. But despite the culture of hate around him—a culture that the man on the side of the road was likely part of—the Samaritan showed compassion by choosing to not generalize his experience of a culture.

The Practice of God's Son

It should not surprise us that Jesus lived out the same attitude of compassionate communication that He taught about in this parable. If anyone had the right to shun an entire people group by avoiding them altogether, Jesus did. The whole human race was enslaved to sin. Since God is completely holy and sinless, He did not have to engage with or save us; He could have left us alone, allowing us to die in our sins and be eternally separated from Him. But He didn't. Instead, He clothed Himself in flesh and pursued us, even when we ran from Him.

Romans 5:6-8 says, "For while we were still weak, at the right time Christ died for the ungodly. For one will scarcely die for a righteous person—though perhaps for a good person one would dare even to die—but God shows his love for us in that while we were still sinners, Christ died for us." God's love is unfailing—in contrast to the limited and often conditional love of humans. In His love, God proactively demonstrated compassion toward us.

While we were sinners, Jesus chose to demonstrate His love for us. He chose to step into our world and become a suffering servant who knew many sorrows; He volunteered to die in our place on the cross. God could have easily and rightfully distrusted the entire human race, but Jesus did not profile us. His perfect love for us would not allow Him to.

The Prescription for God's Saints

And so, as followers of Jesus, we must mirror His example. Let's take a hard look at the prejudice toward people of different ethnicities that is in our hearts. It should not take a video of an unarmed African American man or woman being shot to cause us to confess our personal prejudice. It should not take pictures of children crying after being separated from their parents at the US-Mexican border to compel us to confess the xenophobia hidden behind the idol of comfort in our hearts. It should never have taken the #MeToo #ChurchToo movement for us to recognize and deal with abuse, misogyny, and sexism in the church.

God is calling His church in America to proactively confess the ugly, sinful realities that have been comfortably nestled in our hearts for years. We must cry out alongside the psalmist, "Search me, O God, and know my heart! Try me and know my thoughts! And see if there be any grievous way in me, and lead me in the way everlasting" (Psalm 139:23-24). Let us beg God to surface any sin that we are ignoring, either in ignorance or on purpose. And we must intentionally allow other believers to call out our sin and hold us accountable to bear fruits of repentance.

This is not an impossible task. As Romans 8:9-13 tells us, God the Holy Spirit provides us with the power to put to death the misdeeds of our flesh. This means that every born-again Christian has no excuse for walking in continual wickedness. If we truly want to be free from sins that have ensnared us or encumbrances that are weighing us down, we must proactively ask God to compassionately show us the areas of our lives that grieve Him and cause us to walk out of step with the gospel. We must then be willing to participate in meaningful relationships with an ethnically, generationally, and socioeconomically diverse accountability group of believers who will love us enough to call out our sin and encourage us to repent.

COMPASSION IN OUR COMMUNITIES

Finally, we move toward ethnic conciliation when we work to make the compassion of Christ visible in our communities. Only in active compassion will we end the hostility between Christians from different ethnicities. As we do this, we will learn to meet fellow believers with authentic empathy.

The Parable of the Good Samaritan

As He ended the parable of the Good Samaritan in Luke 10:36, Jesus said, "Which of these three, do you think, proved to be a neighbor to the man who fell among the robbers?" Jesus' question got to the heart of the lawyer's motive for asking, "Who is my neighbor?" The condition of the lawyer's heart becomes clear through his response: "The one who showed him mercy" (verse 37).

Three truths become evident from the lawyer's reply. First, his definition of *neighbor* wasn't in harmony with God's definition. The priest and the Levite would have been the people the lawyer loved—they fit the demographic of who the religious elite classified as their neighbor. Second, he had deep prejudice in his heart: He refused to even acknowledge a Samaritan as the hero of the story. Third, he did not possess eternal life because he didn't love God or his neighbor. Every image bearer is our neighbor. Loving God holistically naturally produces a holistic love for our fellow image bearers. And compassion is the concrete expression of that love.[7] If we lack love and compassion toward others, we lack love for God.

The Practice of God's Son

Jesus' work destroyed the wall of ethnocentricity that kept Jews and Gentiles segregated. Ephesians 2:17-18 says, "He came and preached peace to you who were far off and peace to those who were near. For through him we both have access in one Spirit to the Father." Peace means an absence of animosity, distrust, and hatred. The finished work of Jesus provided eternal peace between God and all sinners who embrace Jesus as Savior—both those who were near (Jews) and those who were far (Gentiles).

Back in the day before cell phones had GPS, Elicia and I invited two families over for barbecue. We provided each family with our home address, and they printed out directions from MapQuest. We soon got a phone call from the first family; they had pulled over to a gas station and called our home from a pay phone. As the husband described their location, we realized that they were only a few blocks away from our house. The route would be confusing to someone not from our neighborhood, however, so I told them to stay where they were, drove to find them, and guided them to our home.

Then the second family called. They were three exits down the freeway and couldn't figure out how to get to us. I told them to stay there, and I drove to find them—fifteen minutes away—so they could follow me back to our home. When we arrived, we enjoyed a great time of fellowship and some of Kansas City's best barbecue.

One family was near and the other was far, and they both lost their way. I had to leave my home to find them and lead them to my house. This is a picture of the gospel's esperanza. Jesus left the comfort of His home in heaven to search out those who were "near"—those who were ethnically Jewish. The Jews were God's chosen people and had stewarded God's Word. Jesus walked among them to pay for their sin and bring them into God's family. Those who were "far" were the Gentiles—people of every other ethnicity. Jesus preached the same gospel truth to them, and He leads those who follow Him to the household of faith (the church).

We see this truth—that Jesus' compassionate sacrifice is offered for the sins of those near and far—in Ephesians 4:4-6: "There is one body and one Spirit—just as you were called to the one hope that belongs to your call—one Lord, one faith, one baptism, one God and father of all, who is over all and through all and in all." Jesus has gathered both Jews and Gentiles to Himself—saving them and building one new humanity, the church. The family of God is made up of people from every nation, tribe, and tongue. Jesus has no prejudice in His presence or practice, and neither should any of His followers.

The Prescription for God's Saints

In Matthew 28:19-20, Jesus commissions His followers to make disciples of every ethnicity—not only in Jerusalem but also in Judea, in Samaria, and all over the world. In the United States of America, God has brought the nations to live in many of the neighborhoods in our cities, yet many churches—in both laity and leadership—do not reflect the demographic of their immediate community. This doesn't mean churches should manufacture diversity if the surrounding community lacks it. But if the demographics of the community start changing, the local church should begin prayerfully diversifying their high-level leadership to reflect the new diversity of their transitioning community.

I'm not only speaking to churches led by those of European descent; I'm speaking to any church in a transitioning community. I've spoken with Spanish-speaking pastors about the need to hire qualified leaders of the ethnicity that is moving into their community. Some established African American pastors, dealing with gentrification in inner-city communities, are looking to hire a pastor of European descent because of the recent change in demographics.

If we as the body of Christ are going to participate in ethnic conciliation, our churches should first assess our understanding of the imago dei by asking whether we see all people from each of the ethnicities in our community as equal image bearers of God—and whether our actions communicate what we say we believe. If not, we must confess our sin of partiality and our supremacist views, renounce them, and repent for not loving our neighbors. We must also realize God has sovereignly determined the nations to land in our neighborhood (Acts 17:24-26).

Next, pastors must communicate the truth of John 1:12-13: that salvation is not a result of one's ethnicity, fleshly will, or personal desires but rather is a gift from God. Consistently communicating this truth will refute the ethnocentric cults that have capitalized on the church's blind spot to partiality for over a century and a half. Pastors must shepherd their people and lead them well by helping them understand that, according to Romans 1:16-17, the gospel transcends all cultures and ethnicities. No one ethnicity, denomination, gender, or social class holds a monopoly on the gospel. The church must steward the message of hope so that all people from all nations may hear of God's plan of redemption in ways they can understand and be given an opportunity to embrace Jesus as Savior.

Lastly, the church must strive to embody Galatians 3:26-28. The local church should show no economic, ethnic, or gender favoritism. If Jesus saves sinners from every nation, tribe, tongue, gender, and socioeconomic class, the church should be a community of the diverse, representing each of these demographics in our communities where they live, move, and have their being. When both leadership and laity of the local church embody this passage, the gospel's power is visibly displayed.

PEOPLE OF COMPASSION

God is calling His church in America to lead a solution-based conversation about the ethnic tensions in our culture. Ephesians 2:11-22 provides the church with a clear and direct framework: Our positional reality embodies ethnic conciliation. American churches have the opportunity to be a brochure of heaven for their local context. If they can reflect the Kingdom diversity of Revelation 7:9 in real time, they will present an extraordinary preview of the Kingdom that is coming. Imagine the credibility the local church can gain when they display a pathway of functional diversity that could even lead the nonbelieving community to insights on healing and conciliation.

Each of us must pursue God, asking Him to highlight our blind spots so that we can approach ethnic conciliation with open and humble hearts. As we do this, we will move increasingly into Jesus' command to make disciples—not just converts—of every ethnicity around the globe. When the church in America does this, we will be known for our ethnic conciliation.

CHAPTER 4

THE SIN OF PARTIALITY

Where the Church Falls Short

Our God does not show partiality. He expresses compassion, equity, and justice not only to people with whom He has covenanted but also to the whole human race. And God commands those who are in a covenant relationship with Him to represent Him by likewise avoiding partiality—with each other and with all people.

Partiality happens when one person superficially evaluates another person's worth and judges them before getting to know them or their story. We practice partiality when we make judgments about a person's character based on all things external: their accent, clothing, gender, hair, height, tattoos, skin color, etc. and then treat that person as if our judgment is true.

Partiality would not be a sin if it were consistent with God's character. But Scripture shows us clearly: Our God is not a prejudiced God.

Deuteronomy 10:17 says God is "God of gods and Lord of lords, the great, the mighty, and the awesome God, who is not partial and takes no bribe." The people who have been called to represent Him must refrain from showing partiality as well. In verses 18 and 19, God calls Israel to execute justice for the orphans, the widow, and the sojourner—taking care of necessities for those who were not part of His covenant community. If God's people, who receive His love, show love to the vulnerable,[1] the vulnerable will see God's heart: He is willing to embrace them and make them part of His covenant people too. It is through this that, early in Scripture, we see God's heart for His people to include men and women of all ethnicities. We see God's impartiality throughout the Old Testament, as He tells His people to show compassion to the poor to express His care and concern for them.

This command away from partiality is weightier for those who lead God's people. In Malachi 2:1-9, God directly rebukes the priests who despised His instruction. In verse 7, he says, "For the lips of a priest should guard knowledge, and people should seek instruction from his mouth, for he is the messenger of the LORD of hosts." Here, God is saying that leadership in His community sets the tone for the attitude, beliefs, and practices of the community that they lead.

Leaders lead by what they communicate but also how they live. The priests in Malachi's day were not only failing to preach the truth but also failing to live out the truthfulness of God's character and leadership. In verse 9, God says, "I make you despised and abased before all the people, inasmuch as you do not keep my ways but show partiality in your instruction." The priests demonstrated partiality by teaching people what they wanted to hear rather than what God's Word truly says. God is a God of truth, and He communicates truth in love. When we do not communicate the whole counsel of God's truth, but rather, only the parts people want to hear, we are showing partiality.

God's impartial nature is clear in the New Testament, as well. In Matthew 22:15-22, as the Pharisees try to trap Jesus, they butter Him up, saying He expresses truth in His teaching and does not care about anyone's opinion because He is not swayed by appearances. What they are admitting is that Jesus did not show partiality.

The question they tried to trap Him with was about paying taxes to Caesar. The Jews did not like to pay the taxes to Rome because it reminded them that they were under the oppressive rule of the Romans. The Pharisees were hoping to get a binary yes-or-no answer. If Jesus said that He was okay with taxes, then that would allow people to say that He was not for the nation of Israel, that He sided with their oppressor. If Jesus took a stand against taxes, then it could be said that He led a rebellious effort to overthrow Roman rule.

But Jesus knew about the malice in their hearts: "Why put me to the test, you hypocrites? Show me the coin for the tax" (Matthew 22:18-19). Notice that Jesus did not disagree with their correct assessment that He teaches truth and shows no partiality. As God in the flesh, Jesus embodied the characteristics of God seen throughout the Old Testament. And since Jesus is God, He rightly discerned the motivation of those who posed the question. Because of that, He refused to give them the binary response they wanted.

Jesus asked the Pharisees whose image was on the coin. "Caesar's," they responded. And then Jesus masterfully nuanced the paradigm: "Therefore render to Caesar the things that are Caesar's, and to God the things that are God's" (Matthew 22:21). Jesus was simply telling them to pay taxes to the people in power because God had put them in that position—and by doing this, they were obeying God, who is the greater authority.

There is an important truth in this when it comes to partiality. Although Caesar was a pagan oppressor of

God's covenant people, he still bore the image of the God who created him. As with all image bearers, he was to be respected and honored by God's people, even though they disagreed with everything that he stood for. When God's people honor the image bearer who is in authority, they honor God. Jesus challenged God's own people to show no partiality not only when it was convenient but also when it was challenging—because doing so would amaze the people who watched.

The rest of the New Testament expands our understanding of God's impartiality. In Romans 2:1-11, Paul stated that God's judgment on human beings is based not on their ethnicity but on the morality of their lifestyle. God desires to save sinners of every ethnicity. If all of humanity is guilty, and the gospel says God can save sinners from every imaginable background, then neither judgment nor salvation is partial. When sinners reject the message of hope the people of God proclaim, they choose condemnation because God must deal with sin. Since God does not show partiality, every sinner who rejects God's plan of redemption will receive judgment.

In 1 Peter 1:15-17, the apostle Peter wrote, "As he who called you is holy, you also be holy in all your conduct, since it is written, 'You shall be holy, for I am holy.' And if you call on him as Father who judges impartially according to each one's deeds, conduct yourselves with fear throughout the time of your exile." If God is truly holy, then He is separate from all sin. This absolute holiness of God includes everything that He does, says, and thinks. God requires holiness from His people so they can remain in a flourishing relationship with Him. The gospel reminds us that Jesus lived in perfect obedience to God and that when we embrace Christ as Savior, His perfection covers us, and we are considered eternally not guilty in God's eyes (Romans 4–5).

Christians stay in fellowship with God because of Jesus' work, and holy living is possible because Jesus made it possible. Since each of us calls *Father* our God who never shows partiality, we must do the same.

Throughout the testimony of Scripture, God consistently refrains from showing partiality. In our sinfulness and stubbornness, we persistently refuse to reflect His characteristics. So we must take a close look at this sin of partiality. What is it? And what does it look like in the lives of God's people?

THE SIN OF PARTIALITY

On July 13, 2013, George Zimmerman was acquitted in the shooting and death of Trayvon Martin. For many Christians in the United States, this case surfaced concerns about racism in our society and in the church itself. People seemed to choose sides based on whether they acknowledged or denied the existence of systemic racism. The divisive question? *Is racism an individual or an institutional issue?*

As the argument grew, believers became more hateful in their speech toward one another, in person and online. By the time the 2016 election season kicked off, members of the American church seemed to be at war with each other, just as nonbelievers were. When Donald Trump was elected, I watched Christians become more fractured than ever before. The American church was on fire.

Amid this chaos, I began recognizing that we have been approaching the conversation regarding ethnic tensions from the wrong angle. People from both sides of the argument—those who thought individual racism was the issue and those who thought institutional racism was the issue—have used shooting statistics to bolster their position, producing a stalemate. But if we as believers wrestle with this issue in light of the sin of partiality, each of us—regardless of ethnicity, gender, political affiliation, social class, or stance on individual versus institutional racism—must examine our hearts. If we examine ourselves through God's Word, allowing the Holy Spirit to surface and convict us of sin, we will be moved to confession and repentance. As this happens on an individual level, we'll see institutional fruits of repentance that will allow the American church to gain social credibility and give a biblical public witness because we are stewarding the gospel in addressing one of America's most foundational sins.

To understand the sin of partiality more thoroughly, let's look at James 2:

> My dear brothers and sisters, how can you claim to have faith in our glorious Lord Jesus Christ if you favor some people over others?
>
> For example, suppose someone comes into your meeting dressed in fancy clothes and expensive jewelry, and another comes in who is poor and dressed in dirty clothes. If you give special attention and a good seat to the rich person, but you say to the poor one, "You can stand over there, or else sit on the floor"—well, doesn't this discrimination show that your judgments are guided by evil motives?
>
> Listen to me, dear brothers and sisters. Hasn't God chosen the poor in this world to be rich in faith? Aren't they the ones who will inherit the Kingdom he promised to those who love him? But you dishonor the poor! Isn't it the rich who oppress you and drag you into court? Aren't they the ones who slander Jesus Christ, whose noble name you bear?

Yes indeed, it is good when you obey the royal law as found in the Scriptures: "Love your neighbor as yourself." But if you favor some people over others, you are committing a sin. You are guilty of breaking the law.

For the person who keeps all of the laws except one is as guilty as a person who has broken all of God's laws. For the same God who said, "You must not commit adultery," also said, "You must not murder." So if you murder someone but do not commit adultery, you have still broken the law.

So whatever you say or whatever you do, remember that you will be judged by the law that sets you free. There will be no mercy for those who have not shown mercy to others. But if you have been merciful, God will be merciful when he judges you.

JAMES 2:1-13, NLT

During the infancy of the church, many of the people of God were poor and, as William Barclay wrote, "if a rich man was converted, and did come to the Christian fellowship, there must have been a very real temptation to make a fuss of him, and to treat him as a special trophy for Christ."[2]

James does not beat around the bush. Paying extra attention to the rich person and neglecting the poor person is the sin of partiality. James calls this behavior what it is: evil (verse 4). Partiality is not consistent with the character of God and tarnishes the reputation of the God we represent.

We can and should apply the implications of partiality to all interpersonal relationships, whether differences between us are in economics, culture, ethnicity, education, language, personality, or political affiliation. When we purposefully give extra attention to some people we prefer, we are by default neglecting those we do not. This evil can become so normal in our practice that we won't even understand the reason when it's called out. The flesh is tricky because we're most comfortable around those who are like us.

James reminded his readers that the ones they were neglecting were heirs in the same Kingdom—and gave examples of how to live out Kingdom ethics on this side of eternity. In James 1:9-11, James contrasts the poor with the rich. Poor Christians are seen as socially insignificant; they are not in the center because they're pushed to the margins. In our day, examples of the marginalized in our churches are children, adolescents, the homeless, immigrants and refugees, prison parolees, the unmarried, and women. James argues that these Christians shouldn't be on the margins of church life but should be embraced in the center because they serve as role models for those whom James classifies as rich.

The rich in our day are Christians who regularly have food in their pantry, who have disposable income to go out to eat, have more than a couple of pairs of clothes, and have a place to live with luxuries like indoor plumbing and heating and cooling. Being rich has nothing to do with the Americanized understanding of being wealthy—instead, it means having enough to live comfortably and be embraced socially. Although I am a person of color who has lived in the margins of American society for most of my life, I am rich by James's definition.

Now, being rich, according to James's definition, is not a sin. Seeking employment, reasonable housing, and upward mobility are not sinful, as long as the Christian's identity is not rooted in these pursuits. Neither is it a curse to be poor, according to James's definition. In the church we have both rich and poor, and we all need each other. I, being rich, learn much from my poor brothers and sisters around the world, specifically here in Los Angeles but also in the Global South. My "first-world problems" are not their problems, and their Holy Spirit-driven lifestyle of contentment convicts me of my pursuit of temporary trinkets, which I buy with disposable income. My confession of such practices has led me to repent before my wife and kids. One fruit of repentance we've implemented is sharing what we have with the poor around us. As a family, we sometimes make meals, put them in bags with toiletries, and give them to the homeless around Long Beach. Then we come home and eat the same meal (normally sandwiches, chips, and water) as a reminder to be grateful for God's provision.

I've found that too often in the church, we do not value people the way God values them. We live out the sin of partiality when we neglect the poor. And when we neglect them, we don't think about them. When we don't think about them, they remain nameless faces we speed past daily. We forget the marginalized have a name and a story, and that they are bearers of God's image—image bearers who, in many ways, help us deconstruct our idols of comfort, greed, and privilege.

James follows his rebuke of partiality with a pathway to repentance (James 2:8-9: "If you really fulfill the royal law according to the Scripture, 'You shall love your neighbor as yourself,' you are doing well. But if you show partiality, you are committing sin and are convicted by the law as transgressors").

So what does it mean to love our neighbor as ourselves?

THE GOLDEN RULE

In Matthew 7:12, Jesus says, "So whatever you wish that others would do to you, do also to them, for this is the Law and the Prophets." This famous and convicting command is commonly known as *the Golden Rule*. The verb Jesus uses here is both present and active,[3] which means we must do it now and *keep on* doing it. We must each make our own conscious decision to live in obedience to the Golden Rule.

We practice the Golden Rule when we put the needs of others before our own. In the context of ethnic conciliation, we do this when we refuse to show partiality or neglect people because of their ethnicity. We also practice the Golden Rule when we comfort those who are afflicted (2 Corinthians 1:3-7) rather than trying to factcheck their painful experiences while they're sharing their story. Many people have experienced trauma in this area of ethnic tensions, and, as Diane Langberg once said, "the trauma of this world is one of the primary mission fields of the twenty-first century."[4] Christians of color (African American, Asian, Latino, Middle Eastern, and Native Indigenous) often spend intense energy trying to convince brothers and sisters (of European descent) in the faith that the prejudicial treatment they've received—from both nonbelievers and other Christians—is real and significant. The struggle to be heard and have our experiences seen as valid is painful and traumatic. This is also true for Christian women of color, who spend twice the energy of men both because they are women and because they are not of European descent. As the body of Christ, we must better empathize with those who risk opening up about their trauma, and we must create pathways of healing from within the church, especially for our sisters, who are in need of affirmation and respite care for their whole being.

Now, I am not singling out Christians of European descent for the sin of partiality; I know firsthand that Christians of color are guilty of doing this to their brothers and sisters of European descent, as well as to other Christians of color. I have been guilty of doing this, and in fact, I didn't get called out for it until 2003, when a pastor who loved me enough called out my sin. I've shown partiality not only to my brothers and sisters of European descent but also to other Christians of color, even other Latinos. When I lived in Florida in 2000, some of my Cuban brothers treated me with partiality because I was Mexican. They would make jokes about me selling oranges near the on-ramps of the Central Florida Expressways. I remember retaliating against them as well, siding with my Puerto Rican friends who said that the fairer-skinned Cubans were "white," not Latino—a deep offense. In those instances, I did not practice the Golden Rule. I played the hypocrite. I knew how it felt to be ridiculed by a fellow Latino, yet that didn't stop me from ridiculing others. And this even affected my desire to be around my Cuban brothers, so I ignored them and felt contempt toward them. We were all still teenagers, unable to deal with the trauma of marginalization, so we turned on each other. Rather than comforting each other in our afflictions, we added to one another's pain. Despite these realities, I was a Jesus follower who willingly committed these sins—and I praise God that I was called out and given the chance to repent. By God's grace, this sin is no longer a rhythm in my life, but if I don't proactively steward my heart, my flesh will progressively go back to its old ways. This truth drives me to have a diverse inner circle of men I can walk with in complete vulnerability. My close circle of friends is not made up of Latinos alone but includes people with other ethnicities.

God tells His covenant people to love Him with all they have so that their good vertical relationship with Him will lead to flourishing horizontal relationships with other human beings. When His people refuse to obey God's royal law to love their neighbor, they show partiality and sin. And the sin of partiality destroys the church's public witness.

When we give preferential treatment, we are showing society that some people are superior and others are inferior. We cannot say we are walking in obedience to God if we fail in this area. And in American Protestant churches, we often try to avoid the conversation about partiality by warring with words about individual and institutional racism.

In the secular world, if we claim that other people are

guilty of racism, they can quickly tell us that we do not know the motives of their heart. We can even show them how they are treating one ethnicity as superior and others as inferior, only to have them say we are misinterpreting their actions. But in the church, we can look at the Word of God. Through the power of the Holy Spirit, we can name partiality for what it is, both individually and institutionally in American church settings.

One way we face the sin of partiality in the church is through taking the Lord's Supper seriously. We see the relational importance of the Lord's Supper in 1 Corinthians 11:17-32, when Corinthian Christians were failing to examine themselves before publicly celebrating the Lord's Supper and God disciplined them by causing them to either become sick or weary or to die.

The Lord's Supper is not just a flippant experience we tack on at the end of our church service. It is a deeply meaningful time where God gives us the opportunity to make things right with Him—and perhaps more importantly, with our brothers and sisters in the faith. God calls each of us to examine our hearts in preparation for the Lord's Supper. When we participate, we are saying publicly that, to the best of our ability, our vertical relationship with God is right and our horizontal relationships with our brothers and sisters are right. We must deal with all our unconfessed and unrepented sins during this time of examination, not just the sin of partiality.

If we take seriously God's command to examine ourselves before participating in the Lord's Supper, God will uncover sins that He wants to address. If we are walking rightly in flourishing relationships with God and our brothers and sisters, our conscience will be clear, allowing us to partake in the Lord's Supper. If God does in fact surface obvious sin we're refusing to confess and repent of, we can choose to respond in one of three ways. First, we can listen to the voice of the Lord and seek reconciliation with God and/or our brother or sister in the faith instead of taking the Lord's Supper. Second, if the individual we need to reconcile with is present, we can seek reconciliation in person and then celebrate the Lord's Supper together. Or third, we can choose to ignore God's leading to deal with our sin and continue to disobey while publicly taking the Lord's Supper. This final option is where God seems to step in.

When we biblically call out the sin of partiality, we are correctly framing it as a sin to be resolved to be in a right relationship with God and others. Each individual believer and church, by the power of the Holy Spirit, must engage in its removal. To do this, the church must call out racism for what it truly is: the sin of partiality. When we rename racism as this sin, we as God's people will begin to leverage His character and His Word as our standard for living. For centuries in our country, people have avoided accountability for racism, often because of power structures that were built to protect those who engage in this sin. But God's prescriptive language in Scripture holds us accountable as His people to show no partiality. Every Christian has the responsibility to walk in holiness in their relationships, both vertically and horizontally.

When the sin of partiality is named and the sinning brother or sister does not seek reconciliation, the church has God's permission to seek restoration of the sinning Christian's soul by calling them to repentance. Church discipline is the means of purification, not only for the life practices of Christian but also for the public witness of the church of Jesus Christ. We are to provide mercy when confronting sin, providing a pathway to freedom from what ensnares the heart of our brother or sister. As we do this, God will purge the sin of partiality from both individuals and institutions in the American church, producing the fruits of repentance, restoring relationships, and helping the church regain its societal credibility by resembling the only true and living God.

CALLING OUT PARTIALITY

Calling out the sin of partiality is a daunting task. And as we do this, we must be very aware that the evil one will attempt to cause division among God's people to discredit our public witness, distract us from our mission, and tarnish Christ's reputation. Pain and tension will surface when we call out the sin of partiality—a necessary part of healing an infected wound.

When I was a child, the left side of my knee split open in a bicycle accident. I was too scared to tell my parents, so I went home and bandaged it myself. I tried to put antiseptic on it, then stopped because of the pain. A few days went by—and the hidden untreated cut got infected. When my mom noticed me limping, I lied about hurting my knee so she would stop asking questions. But the next day, I wore shorts, and my mom saw my open wound and confronted me. When she saw how infected the cut was, she took me into the bathroom and compassionately drained it, cleansed it with peroxide, and applied a topical antiseptic. This entire process hurt, but the pain was necessary to get rid of the infection. To this day, I still have a scar from the incident—evidence that healing took place!

Our risen Lord bears scars from the cross. And His incarnational body, the church, needs scars—not infected wounds—to show visible evidence that healing is possible. In America, our wounds are infected, and we've tried to hide the infection from Jesus, our Great Physician, long enough. He wants to heal us, but to start this process, we must risk confession. We must address partiality in our lives and in our communities, as well as among our leaders. And guess what? Jesus is calling us to do today what He called the fathers and mothers of our faith to do well over three millennia ago.

Addressing Partiality among God's People

In Acts 6:1, we read, "In these days when the disciples were increasing in number, a complaint by the Hellenists arose against the Hebrews because their widows were being neglected in the daily distribution." In this passage, Luke unveils the existence of cultural and ethnic tensions—and the brokenness such tensions create—present in the early church.

Remember, in Deuteronomy 10:17-18, we read of God's lack of bias and how He calls His people to reflect His character by executing justice for the fatherless, the widow, and the sojourner. God says that He is the one who provides food and clothing to each of these identified vulnerable groups. God uses His people to meet the needs of the needy.

During the time when Acts 6 was written, there was an established system of support for widows who adhered to Judaism.[5] When a widow embraced Jesus as her Savior, she was no longer permitted to receive the support she once enjoyed because she had abandoned Judaism to follow Jesus. In Acts 2:42-47, we see the church forming a system to care for needs within the body of Christ. But in Acts 6:1, the Hellenists charge the Hebrews with purposely neglecting their widows in the daily distribution. This is not a superficial airing of suspicions; rather, it is calling out sinful actions seen in real time.

In Acts 6:2-4, the twelve apostles called a meeting, inviting believers to discuss this situation. Out of this meeting, the apostles appointed men in the congregation—seven who had good reputations and were full of the Spirit and wisdom—to lead the just distribution of support for all widows, regardless of their culture or language.

In Acts 6:5-6, we learn which men were selected. What's amazing is that each of them had a Greek name—they were Hellenists themselves. The oppressed widows who were not receiving support would now have adequate representation in leadership; these men would be fair not only to the Hellenist widows but also to the Hebrew widows.

The result of this move was that God made His church flourish. Acts 6:7 says, "The word of God continued to increase, and the number of the disciples multiplied greatly in Jerusalem, and a great many of the priests became obedient to the faith." When the church removed partiality, it reflected God's love, compassion, and concern for the needy. The church lived in obedience to God's commands.

We can learn several crucial elements of addressing partiality among God's people from this Scripture. First, we must be able to prove that our brothers and sisters are acting in partiality. Second, we must have hard conversations that expose the sin of partiality and entreat the erring Christian to repent. And third, we must provide a pathway for repentance and restoration alongside that denouncement of sin.

Addressing Partiality among Leadership

It's one thing to correct partiality in church members' lives. It is even more notable and difficult when leaders step up to confront and correct other leaders who have committed the sin of partiality. Perhaps one of the most recognized instances of this in Scripture is when the apostle Paul rebuked the apostle Peter to his face (Galatians 2:11-14). Former pastor and seminary professor Thomas Constable says Paul's rebuke of Peter came publicly because Peter's behavior was casting doubt that God accepted Jews and Gentiles equally.[6]

On first arriving in Antioch, Peter had no problem fellowshipping and sharing meals with Christians who were Gentiles. But when Jews came to Antioch from Jerusalem, he fell back from interacting openly with the Gentiles and then began segregating himself from them altogether. Since Peter was an apostle, he was a leader; the members of the church watched not only his actions but also his example.

Peter's actions contradicted those of Jesus, who

publicly engaged in meaningful dialogue with an out-cast woman (John 4:1-30) and chose to eat with sinners (Luke 15:2). Peter's actions were also out of step with the very gospel that he preached and proclaimed. So Paul personally confronted Peter and called his actions what they were: sin (Galatians 2:11-14).

When Paul describes Peter's actions as out of step with the gospel, he uses wording that indicates something needing to be set straight. The prefix to the Greek word in Galatians 2 that expresses this concept is where we get the English word *orthodontist*. An orthodontist assists people with crooked teeth, placing braces on the teeth to align them and make them straight. When our oldest daughter, Bella, turned twelve years old, we consulted an orthodontist regarding Bella's teeth. After looking at the X-rays, we all agreed that braces were the best option. The orthodontist instructed Bella how to deal with the pain the braces would cause as they began straightening her teeth into alignment.

The orthodontist also provided literature on how Bella's teeth could still be taken care of to prevent decay, disease, and even the discomforts of this correction process. Countless times during this alignment process, Elicia and I comforted Bella in her pain and corrected her when she ate foods that were counterproductive to the correction the braces were providing.

This is what happens in the life of a Christian leader

who has been guilty of the sin of partiality. The gospel brings comfort that the sin is forgiven, but the process of aligning their behavior with God's character can be painful. The embarrassment of publicly confessing sin and walking in repentance is necessary pain, though. When a leader has led others astray in the sin of partiality, the leader must also model repentance and restoration.

NO MORE PARTIALITY

Whenever our behavior contradicts the truth of the gospel, we need to confess our sin and seek to align our life with God's heart. And no one is exempt from the sin of partiality. Each of us must confess our sin and walk in the fruits of repentance. Local church leaders should also proactively seek to restore Christians who practice the sin of partiality, particularly when they're segregating themselves from other Christians because of their ethnicity. In churches where the sin of partiality has deep roots, we must deal with it in accordance to God's Word, calling it out, offering opportunity for people to repent, and corporately working to see leadership of the oppressed ethnicity represented in the congregation.

When Christian leaders exhibit the sin of partiality in their lives, leading others to walk out of step with the gospel, other Christian leaders should call them out. Scripture shows that when leaders confess and repent of sins, people regain a healthy fear of God. The gospel's power is put on display, and the church can gain a strong public witness for God's glory.

In the letter to the Galatians, Paul said, "There is neither Jew nor Greek, there is neither slave nor free, there is no male and female, for you are all one in Christ Jesus" (3:28). God does not show ethnic, socioeconomic, or gender bias when saving sinners. The church must reflect God's heart, refraining from prejudice while sharing the Good News of the gospel of Jesus Christ (1 Corinthians 15:1-4) with sinners from every imaginable walk of life and laboring to meet the needs of the oppressed and afflicted (James 1:27). This is what a hope-filled people can look like as we repent and remove partiality from our churches.

CHAPTER 5

COLOR-BLIND CHRISTIANITY

Introducing the Vital Practice of Affirmation

Paul's words in Galatians 3:28—"There is neither Jew nor Greek, there is neither slave nor free, there is no male and female, for you are all one in Christ Jesus"— are a powerful statement against the sin of partiality, as we talked about in the last chapter. But they have also been misused in our conversations about ethnicity. I've noticed that many evangelicals use this verse as a mute button for conversations dealing with ethnic tensions—as if when they quote it, the ethnicity of believers somehow dissolves, and we just see people as Christian without any ethnic heritage.

The statement usually goes like this: "When I look

at people, I don't see color; I see souls who need Jesus."
When someone says this to me, I ask how they see their
brothers and sisters in Christ who are of a different
ethnicity. The common response is sincere: "I'm color
blind. I don't see color, I only see Christ." The irony is
that this is usually—though not always—said by evangelicals of European descent.

There is a difference between the sin of partiality and
what I call *Christian color blindness*. Partiality can be
hidden deeply in the heart, making it harder to call out,
while Christian color blindness is usually expressed freely
and sincerely. In my personal experience, when I engage
in conversations on ethnicity, a response of Christian
color blindness does more harm than good. Christian
color blindness is when *professing believers in Christ use
a Jesus Juke*[1] *to ignore other image bearers' ethnicity instead
of affirming it*. At the core of my soul, I believe that
people who profess Christian color blindness do so with
a sincere heart, hoping for unity in the body of Christ,
and that they are unaware of the detriment of stripping
the beautiful diversity of the body—the unique ways
different ethnicities exhibit God's image—in the name
of unity. Unity is not the same as conformity—and
Christian color blindness suggests that conformity is
what is required for people of color to be a harmoni-
ous part of the body of Christ. When the people saying they are color blind are leaders of institutions, the

institution likely lacks the diversity in leadership that projects Kingdom representation.

I am a Christian who is Latino, and Christian color blindness stings my heart. It goes against God's intention for ethnic diversity, and it's an attempt to avoid needed conversations about ethnic diversity inside of the body of Christ, especially within evangelicalism. We don't need to put a gag order on these talks. We need to holistically deal with our ethnicity issues so that ethnic conciliation becomes evident in our denominational structures, higher-academic institutions, conference lineups, pastoral teams, and interpersonal relationships. If the church is to reflect God's character, we must ask ourselves a crucial question: *Is God color blind?*

GOD IS NOT COLOR BLIND

God has created every human being in His image (Genesis 1:26-27), which means that we share snapshots of His character that no other creatures carry. Humans are God's crowning act of creation.

The human race includes a multitude of ethnicities that God created out of His genius and for His glory. Ethnic diversity was God's idea. He has the patent on it and has licensed His church to do marketing for it. God didn't create us all the same, and He shows no partiality toward one ethnicity over another (Acts 10:34). It is

God's design that we will retain our ethnicities eternally (Revelation 7:9). And since the church is a preview of heaven, it is no accident that Jesus Christ, God in the flesh, commanded His followers to make disciples of every ethnic heritage (Matthew 28:19-20).

Knowing the sinfulness of man and how we long to segregate ourselves based on comfort and preferences, God saw the need to include in His Word insights about how, as His body, we are to personify unity without mandating uniformity. Christ has broken down all walls of hostility to offer salvation to people from every ethnicity (Ephesians 2:11-22). God draws sinners to Christ for salvation regardless of ethnicity (Romans 1:16-17; 10:9-17).

It's obvious that God is not color blind. So how can so many Christians say that they are?

ETHNICITY IN EVANGELICALISM

On many occasions when I've taught about ethnic conciliation, I've received pushback from people who fear that I'm advocating ethnocentrism—proclaiming one ethnicity superior to all others. In these conversations, people ask me to give ample Scripture to support my claims. When I do that, they then ask me to provide statistical data. After I comply, they tell me I'm being bitter and one-sided. Please hear my heart when I say this: When it comes to any topic of Scripture—in this case, ethnicity—it's not about *how much* Bible you use but *how* you use the Bible.

To unpack what I mean by that, let's look at Galatians 3:28. Essentially, Paul is explaining how Christ's work provides all believers with an equal position in God's family. People rarely argue with this understanding. As I mentioned earlier, however, many people quote this passage to shut down conversations about ethnic tensions in the body of Christ, as if it's a panic button.

While on a panel at the Legacy Conference,[2] Professor Soong-Chan Rah brought out an interesting yet often overlooked truth of this passage. He asked, essentially, "If Christians are not expected to turn off their gender or their status of employment when they are saved, why are they being asked to turn off their ethnicity?" His words made me think back to when I was saved. At the moment of my regeneration, I was justified, indwelt by the Spirit of God, and a recipient of Christ's imputed righteousness *positionally*. Yet *practically*, I remained an ethnic minority, male, and economically in the lower class. Over the course of time, evangelicalism affirmed all of my positional reality but only two-thirds of my practical reality: my gender and my socioeconomic position.

In evangelicalism, I have never been challenged to live a gender-blind or socioeconomic-blind life. But when it comes to ethnicity, evangelical Christians of European descent often call people of other ethnicities to turn off that part of their identity to function in a delusional, color-blind church. That is not in step with the gospel, nor is it the best way forward.

A BROWN RESPONSE

As I've read and assessed voices of various colors who have responded to the normalizing of what is called "white evangelicalism," I can understand each side of the argument. I myself am asked to speak at many events hosted and promoted by organizations led by . . . well, evangelicals of European descent. This has helped me build relationships with executive decision-making leaders of denominations, networks, seminaries, and universities, and I have strong, solid friendships with leaders of European descent inside evangelicalism. These relationships have given me the opportunity for many candid conversations about ethnicity, paternalism, and the checkered past of evangelicalism as it relates to the treatment of men and women who are not fully of European descent. Out of these conversations, people have mobilized to more intentionally invest in educational opportunities and financial support for nonwhite Christians and the ministries they're leading. Over time, I've also seen structural leadership changes in evangelical organizations as leaders who are not of European descent are installed in high-level leadership positions.

These experiences have led me to a few convictions about how we can walk forward well in addressing color blindness in evangelicalism.

First, we must have a proper perspective about evangelicalism itself and the people on all sides of it. It is Christ's work that saves, not the term *evangelical*. When Christians of non-European descent depart from the "white evangelical machine," they're not departing from the Christian faith. Neither are evangelicals of European descent enemies of Jesus.

Second, if we are willing to face the reality of harmful color blindness, we must each pursue intentional steps to rid ourselves of this mentality: We must engage in intellectual equipping; we must develop rhythms of ongoing interpersonal engagement; and we must develop interdependent endurance with those of different ethnic backgrounds with whom we are in meaningful relationships.

Intellectual Equipping

The culture at large often charges evangelicals with not thinking critically. And I think there is merit to this claim—particularly when it comes to how we engage with our various ethnicities and the systemic brokenness in the church and in society. In evangelicalism, many of our conversations are not multiethnic because we lack diversity among our leaders and influencers. We must learn to humble ourselves by listening to other Christians, both men and women, who differ from us culturally, ethnically, politically, and theologically.

We cannot think critically if we're only hearing one side of the conversation—which happens when we purposely exclude differing voices from the dialogue. I'm reminded of a time when a prominent evangelical pastor once blogged about police officers who are of European descent but patrol in predominately African American communities. The pastor, who is of European descent, deferred to a police officer, also of European descent, who shared his experience. The pastor said he wrote the piece to challenge Christians to think more critically about the sensitive issue of involving such police officers serving in predominately African American communities. But how could he or his readers think critically when only one side of the argument was given? The best thing the pastor could have done would have been to also feature insights from African American voices (including men and women) from the very community the officer patrolled. In these difficult conversations, it's crucial to share both vantage points.

Perhaps the pastor lacked personal relationships that would have equipped him to seek out the qualified African American view. If any of us face this kind of lack, we must seek out opportunities to learn from people who are different from us by reading and listening to them. While we're hearing new things from fresh voices, we must also become better disciplined in our study of God's Word so we can filter what we're listening to and reading. In doing this, we will develop a gospel-saturated lens through which we can filter the voices of our culture.

With this filter in place, we can and should diversify the voices we listen to, reading authors of color, both male and female, who are wrestling with the social constructs inside and outside evangelicalism. We can each make the personal decision to, at bare minimum, begin reading books from authors who are different from us. We can go to Vimeo or YouTube and listen to sermons, conference talks, and academic lectures from people whose life experiences differ from our own. During our commutes, we can listen to podcasts from people who are both educated and passionate about issues in which we lack understanding. All of these choices can be done in the privacy of our own homes and on our own phones.

Interpersonal Engagement

The next crucial step is to invite—in real ways and into our personal spaces—people who are different from us so we can begin developing meaningful personal relationships with them. This gives us an opportunity to process what we've been reading and listening to with believers from different ethnic backgrounds. As existing conflicts are unveiled through our dialogue, the superficial, touch-and-go level of our relationships will be deconstructed.

We evangelicals must understand that conflict itself is not bad: It's the litmus test identifying the level of depth in our relationships. What *is* bad is abandoning conflict without biblically resolving it. I want to challenge each of us: Do not abandon the interethnic relationships you start building with your brothers and sisters in Christ, no matter what level of despair, disagreement, and frustration you face. Abandonment is destructive to the flourishing God has designed for His body, and when we resort to such a practice, we're out of step with the Spirit (Galatians 5:16-26). And for ethnic-minority evangelicals, relational abandonment crushes our souls. Many of us paid the admission fee into evangelicalism of exhausting our indigenous social capital. If we're abandoned during times of relationship building, where do we, who have no homogenous ecclesiological enclaves, go?

Here's what I mean by "no homogenous ecclesiological enclave." A major evangelical conference promoted their event around the theme "We are Protestant"—yet the main-stage speaker lineup was made up of men of European descent, except for my dear brother Thabiti Anyabwile. All other speakers of color (African

American, Asian, and Latino) were teaching breakouts that dealt with their "African American," "Asian,"
and "Hispanic" nuances. When I saw this branding, I
immediately had three questions. First, were there any
people of non-European descent in the marketing and
strategy meetings who could have said, "What does
our speaker lineup reflect—the Kingdom of God or
American evangelicalism?" Second, was nobody present
to ask the executive leadership, "Are we not continuing
to stereotype Christians of color by not only not having
them speak in general sessions (the center) but also causing them to fellowship and teach theology in breakouts
(the margins)?" And third, I thought, *If there's no brown
representation in any of the branding, are I and my* gente
*not Protestant, and should we then go back to the Roman
Catholic church?*

I've had numerous conversations with Christians
of color who, feeling rejected and unrepresented by
American evangelicalism, simply leave. In the evangelical space, our needs are not considered, which leads us
to believe that we're not wanted. Where do these exiles
go? Some move into de-evangelicalized spaces, remaining committed to orthodoxy but removing themselves
from the woes of an American or European evangelical framework. Some choose ecumenicalism or spiritual isolation, and others go into ethnocentric heretical
movements that affirm their ethnic identity. These

ethnocentric movements (such as the Hebrew Israelites, Moorish Science Temple, Nation of Gods and Earths, and the Nation of Islam) call Christians of non-European descent to move from the "white man's religion" to one that embraces—and ultimately, idolizes—their ethnicity. When challenging and tense times arise, we must love brothers and sisters of non-European descent better—personifying the "one anothers"[3] articulated in Scripture and relying on the empowerment of the Holy Spirit, who indwells us (Romans 8:9-13) to bear each other's burdens (Galatians 6:2) for the long haul.

One of the best ways we can begin developing interpersonal relationships with these brothers and sisters is to make the conscious decision to diversify our dinner tables. Something special takes place when the people of God share meals. At the dinner table, we're all professing our common humanity, our need for nourishment. We should begin our times together by giving thanks to our good God who has provided all good and perfect gifts to us (James 1:17). Then we enjoy each other's company, sharing our lives with each other. The hosts must be willing to open their home as well as their lives to the ones they're working to build meaningful relationships with. And the conversations that start at the dinner tables can and should remain ongoing as each person or family takes turns hosting. (Entering into each other's spaces provides greater opportunity for empathy and understanding.) This commitment to continued relationship allows believers to gain a more in-depth understanding of one another's stories.

Relationships are risky, but the reward of togetherness far outweighs the risk. How can you reach out to the diverse family of God in concrete ways? If you feel that inviting someone into your home is too intrusive a first step, perhaps you can invite someone to go out to lunch with you after a worship service. Carving out that time will help each of you lay some initial relational groundwork. If things go well, then inviting that person to your home could be the next step.

I know—it can be awkward and intimidating to try to start conversations with people you're just getting to know. I lean on my wife's strengths in this area; God has blessed her with the gift of hospitality and the ability to shape meaningful conversations. But we have both chosen to be present and engaged in these conversations, no matter the discomfort. By God's grace, we have been blessed to see the nations enter every home we've lived in.

To start meaningful dialogue, ask open-ended questions that provide everyone at the table an opportunity to unveil a little bit more about their story. If you are hosting other believers, one of the first obvious questions is how they came to know the Lord Jesus Christ. Another is to simply ask them to share their story, where they grew up, experiences that they feel comfortable enough to share, and maybe their reason for living in your community.

As the relationship continues to deepen, you will establish greater levels of trust, perhaps allowing for more meaningful dialogue about ethnic and cultural differences. This is where it is crucial to have soft ears and hearts and a willingness to express empathy. As you enter the water of tense conversations, allow yourself to receive the emotions and stories that might surface. Develop a balance of listening and learning, all while creating an environment of honesty and safety, making sure that each of you know you do not have to agree on every nuance of opinion. When both people or families desire to pursue the relationship despite disagreement, the relationship grows stronger.

Healthy disagreements provide a framework of freedom in a relationship. Often, when things go too well, we fear a land mine that we have somehow been able to avoid so far but will eventually blow up the relationship. If we have disagreements early on and still pursue togetherness, the relationship can grow in safety and freedom.

Often it is said in America that we should avoid talking to each other about politics and religion. If you are a Christian who is in love with Christ and who is socially conscientious, you might be tempted to laugh off this cliché. And yes, in an environment of mutual respect and trust, you can broach difficult topics. But there is wisdom in picking and choosing who you have political conversations with and what topics are up for discussion.

Sharing meals and conversations with people from different backgrounds is profoundly important for this work of ethnic conciliation. When I sit across the table from a law-enforcement officer who feels profiled because of his badge and uniform, I gain a new level of empathy for law-enforcement officers and first responders everywhere. Likewise, when they are willing to hear about my personal experiences of discrimination from law-enforcement officers, they have a new level of empathy for someone who has faced discrimination based on how he was dressed, how he talked, or the county of residence on his license plate. Consistent and ongoing interpersonal engagement brings with it affirmation of the ethnic identity of people who mean much to us—and a better ability to work together and empathize moving forward.

Interdependent Endurance

Once we decide to fight for a meaningful relationship with the brother and sister whose ethnicity is different from ours, together, we'll naturally allow the agape love of God to serve as our "bond of peace" (Ephesians 4:1-6).

This is God's design for interpersonal relationships in the body of Christ: that we would fully know and fully love each other and remain faithful in our commitment to each other. Our peace is not the absence of conflict; rather, working together to achieve peace amid conflict will form a strong bond between believers. This bond will not be broken by disagreements or miscommunication. When the world sees peace among the mosaic of colors, genders, generations, and socioeconomic classes that make up the local church, they should long for what we have. We then can invite them to become part of God's family.

During times of local, national, or global disturbance, we turn toward those we know and trust for comfort. Sometimes in Scripture, we see the Lord allowing tragedy to be a tool for developing oneness in the body of Christ. Physical and social persecution pushed the church to make disciples of all people around the globe, not just of Jews living in Jerusalem. Throughout church history, we see the church caring for the needs of their own, regardless of gender, ethnicity, or social class amid trial: plagues, martyrdom, and even more personal moments such as unemployment. These are the countercultural roots of our faith, stemming back to the pre-Constantine era, when the church looked less like a business and more like a family.[4]

THE WAY OF AFFIRMATION

If we seek to remove Christian color blindness—and we must—we will affirm the ethnicity of every believer rather than acquiescing to or absolving it. Affirmation is the balance between idolizing and ignoring. Idolizing a person's ethnicity results in ethnocentricity. Ignoring it is color blindness. Neither is supported in Scripture, so Christians should reject both. Affirmation takes place when a person acknowledges and celebrates their ethnic identity and when others—when we—acknowledge and celebrate it also. As we individually remove color blindness from our hearts and homes by intellectually equipping ourselves, building interpersonal relationships, and operating with interdependent endurance, we will tangibly present our culture with a foretaste of God's final plan of redemption (Revelation 5:9; 7:9; 21). And we will be walking in obedience to Christ's command to make disciples from every ethnicity (Matthew 28:19-20).

CHAPTER 6

TANGIBLE REPENTANCE

Walking Alongside the Marginalized

Racism has been called America's original sin. Theologian Jim Wallis argues that "our original racial diversity was a product of appalling human oppression based on greed."[1] And I agree with him that greed is America's deeper original sin. The doctrine of discovery, which I mentioned earlier, was rooted in greed. Identifying greed as America's original sin provides more clarity about the motives behind the genocide inflicted on indigenous nations present before colonization and the transatlantic slave trade. And in the church, because people argue around the topic of racism, it's more effective to call out specific sins that are biblically identifiable, like greed and the sin of partiality.

When we embrace Jesus as Savior, all our sins have been forgiven, washed away by His shed blood (Ephesians 1:7). But some of the grievous sins we have committed—both before and after we were saved—still bear consequences. Jesus will not make all things new until we are with Him in the City of God. Until then, we must intentionally seek closure, reconciliation, and reparation for the sins we have committed. We must also take into consideration the sins previous generations of Jesus followers committed here in America, especially when we're dealing with people from different ethnic groups.

This is where the conversation gets challenging and our inconsistency regarding the corporate body of Christ and individualism shows. Often in America, our virtue of individualism causes us to read individuality into the Bible. Many of us have been trained to look for what we can get out of Scripture rather than what God intended to communicate: a love letter to all of His people. Instead of reading and living in an individualistic mind-set, we must bear in mind our corporate reality as the body of Christ, the passing down of systems and traditions from one generation to the next. These systems and traditions are not always inherently sinful, but since systems are created and maintained by people who are prone to sin, wickedness can go unchecked for generations. Wickedness remains until generational leaders name it, repent of it, and seek to bear fruits of repentance going forward.

We see current examples of this in American church denominations and networks where things like abuse of power in leadership and systemic sexual abuse are coming to light. Many leaders who did not directly participate in these sins show courage and repentance by confessing sins, apologizing to the congregation, sharing how sinning leaders will be held accountable (and spiritually restored), seeking forgiveness from offended parties, and creating a pathway forward highlighted by fruits of repentance. The fruits of repentance are not just heartfelt apologies but action steps providing healing for victims, new guardrails for internal policies, and an awareness of how deeply people have been hurt by the system. The longer the systemic abuse, the deeper the wounds, and the more complicated healing will be.

Too often, we're tempted to use individualism as the get-out-of-jail-free card when corporate issues arise. But in the body of Christ, we are a *body*. If my lungs are infected with pneumonia, my other organs can't jump out of my body simply because one part is infected. In fact, if my immune system is healthy and all the parts of my body are working together, my body can fight off the infection. If my immune system is weak, then the infection wins, and it can be fatal if left untreated.[2] Similarly, the sins of greed and partiality have infected Christ's body in America. When we ignored the Holy Spirit–inspired prophetic voices—our immune system— speaking out against the generational sins of racism and hatred, the infection spread throughout the body. Over the course of time, this infection has weakened the immune system. Jesus is the head of the body, and we will not face death. But by refusing to rid ourselves of inherited sinful systems and refusing to get to the root of the infection—greed and partiality—we have been working against Jesus' desire to heal His body.

In the American church, the sins of greed and partiality practiced in previous generations against fellow image bearers need to be dealt with more comprehensively than written resolutions that acknowledge obvious sins in our past. A person with pneumonia shouldn't only recount lifestyle choices that weakened their immune system or keep rehashing their symptoms! Eventually, the patient needs to seek medical attention and utilize the proper prescription, diet, and rest needed to regain health. We, the body of Christian America, must seek the medical attention of our Great Physician, Jesus, who desires to heal us from the consequences of sinful decisions in our national church history. And His prescription is repentance and making amends for our systemic and generational sin.

The mandate and example of making amends for sin is throughout Scripture, and it's helpful to examine these statements and stories in order to understand how to respond to the treatment of people, such as the forced relocation of indigenous nations to reservations during the Trail of Tears, the treatment of African slaves (not just with chattel slavery but also the treatment of their descendants through Jim Crow), the wrongful displacement of landowning Mexican Americans during Manifest Destiny at the hands of Christians, the forced relocation of Japanese Americans to concentration camps during World War II, and the US ban against Chinese immigrants enforced by the Chinese Exclusion Act. In the Old Testament, God made it clear that His people were to seek reparation for sins against others. Leviticus 5:15-17 highlights the guilt or repatriation offerings for sin, and as does Leviticus 6:1-7, which speaks directly to a person who willfully sinned against another. Numbers 5:6-7 says,

> Speak to the people of Israel, When a man or woman commits any of the sins that people commit by breaking faith with the LORD, and that person realizes his guilt, he shall confess his sin that he has committed. And he shall make full restitution for his wrong, adding a fifth to it and giving it to him to whom he did the wrong.

Here, God is telling His covenant people to make things right with the people they have wronged. Thomas Constable says that sins against one's neighbor (as Jesus tells us in Luke 10:25-37, our neighbor is any fellow human being) needed to be atoned for because they "constituted acts of 'unfaithfulness' to God [Leviticus 6:6]. The Israelites had to maintain proper *horizontal* relationships with their neighbors—in order to maintain a proper *vertical* relationship with Yahweh (cf. Matt. 5:23-24)."[3]

If we turn to the New Testament, we see Jesus engaging with reparations as part of repentance (Luke 19:1-10). In summary, Zacchaeus was a tax collector who was taking more than he was required, enriching himself on the backs of the impoverished and struggling around him. What's interesting is that when Jesus called Zacchaeus into relationship, Zacchaeus made a public profession of repentance that included doing more than the law required. His profession to make full restitution showed that he was repentant! He did not just offer an apology—he put his money where his mouth was, and where his sins were too.[4]

Some of you might be tempted to write off what I'm saying—"Oh, but that was for sins Zacchaeus committed directly" or "The Old Testament law isn't something we have to follow because we're under the new covenant." But these excuses miss the heart of God. God's heart throughout Scripture is for reconciliation and repentance, and repentance is active. He also talks about generational sin many times in the Old Testament (e.g., Exodus 34:7; Numbers 14:18), and Psalm 79:8-9 indicates that repentance is also generational. In evangelical spaces, there seems to be no struggle with viewing the sin of abortion as corporate, even when anti-abortion individuals have never committed one. I've been in prayer services where pastors and leaders confess the corporate, national sin of abortion, cry out in repentance, and plead with God to extend forgiveness. What I do not see is this same fervor given toward greed and partiality; somehow, these are viewed as individual, not systemic, sins.

To see what living out the commands of Scripture looks like as we pursue ethnic conciliation, let's review a modern example. Adam Thomason made me aware of this story, and it pierced my heart. In 1838, Georgetown University facilitated a horrific sale of slaves—the Jesuit priests and former presidents who oversaw the Catholic institution sold them to keep it open for business. The sale of 272 human lives—for "about $3.3 million in today's dollars"—secured the future of operations for Georgetown University.[5] When this history came to light, one of the school's alumni, Richard J. Cellini, was moved to repentant action. He started a nonprofit, hired eight genealogists, and was able to raise more than ten thousand dollars from fellow alumni to track down living descendants of the slaves who had been sold.[6]

Georgetown's president John J. DeGioia issued a formal apology and expressed a desire to atone for the past. First, the two buildings named after the former presidents were renamed: "one for an enslaved African-American man and the other for an African-American educator who belonged to a Catholic religious order."[7] The descendants of the slaves will be given preferred status in their admissions applications. The families of the sold slaves are asking the school to do more in a tangible expression that makes amends.[8]

This entire situation is complex. In the sale of these 272 image bearers, families were separated, children were taken from their parents, and they were all shipped from Maryland to Louisiana. These precious souls were leveraged as a commodity to keep the lights on at an academic institution—a religious one, at that. The alumni and president in 2016 had not participated in the sale of the slaves, but they were moved to act because they benefited, unwittingly, from this past evil.

Perhaps this is a cue American Protestants can learn from. Consider all the church buildings, parsonages, universities, and seminaries that have been built on stolen land and paid for by free slave labor. Would it be too farfetched to hire genealogists to dig into the history, and for us to consider what tangible repentance and mercy might look like?

In the next chapter, I will give some corporate

considerations for what making amends can look like. But in this chapter, I want to first challenge you. If you recall, it was an individual, not an organization, who first stood up to seek to make amends at Georgetown. Richard J. Cellini didn't participate in selling humans, but he realized that as a member of the alumni of Georgetown, he could help make things right. It is one thing to offer an apology; it is another to walk in the fruits of repentance. We are talking about millions of people impacted. We are talking about generational wounds that have never healed, centuries-old infected scars on family trees. What would it look like if we, as the people of God, sought to work toward ethnic con-ciliation through this kind of active repentance?

Jesus' response to Zacchaeus's active repentance and restitution was bringing salvation to his home *that day*. Practicing obedience to God's commandments made Zacchaeus a true spiritual child of Abraham, not just one who shared his ethnicity. In Luke 19:10, Jesus said that His mission was to seek and save the lost—not only those who were present and in the center of society but also those who were on its margins. Jesus acted with compassion while ministering to the marginalized of the society in which He lived.

In the United States today, ministry among the marginalized is how we can pursue reconciliation and live in active repentance for generational sins. But often in these ministries, I see a gap between the church and its context. If we seek to push back the darkness and participate in ethnic conciliation, we must pursue a Jesus-centered understanding of mercy in our presuppositions, audience, and intercession.

MARGINALIZED PRESUPPOSITIONS (MATTHEW 9:36)

If we seek to pursue ethnic conciliation and to find places of active repentance, we must first examine our presuppositions. When we bring a marginalized presupposition to our ministry, we see people as projects. A Jesus-centered view of mercy leads us to instead treat all people with compassion. We should never forget that every human being is an image bearer of the God who created them. People are people. They should never be seen as merely projects or statistics. When we reduce them to that, we are stripping the imago dei away from them.

The church can reestablish a strong gospel witness if we show that all people have dignity and value given to them by our common Creator. We can then run to them and consistently live with mercy toward them, just as we saw Jesus do.

Matthew says that when Jesus saw the crowds, He had compassion for them (9:36). Let's take a minute to reflect on that statement again. Crowds pursued Jesus because He made Himself available to them. He was not preoccupied with other things that would distract Him from seeing people. We often get caught up in the everyday routines of life and pass by countless people we're too preoccupied to even see, but living out the mercy of Jesus means stepping out of our routines and choosing to see and care about the individuals around us.

As I mentioned in chapter 3, when Jesus saw the crowds, His every move was with compassion. Every day while He was preaching and healing, Jesus saw every face in the crowd as a valued treasure, not as a roadblock to finishing a task. Jesus had this compassion because the people "were harassed and helpless, like sheep without a shepherd" (Matthew 9:36). The words *harassed* and *helpless* help us understand that Jesus had compassion on people who were being mistreated, neglected, and abused. They were marginalized and vulnerable, being bullied—and the ones delivering this systemic abuse were the religious leaders of Jesus' day. The religious leaders should have been distributing mercy, but they were more concerned with creating a system that benefited them and their peers (Ezekiel 34:1-4). God was not pleased with this system, and throughout the incarnational ministry of Jesus, He regularly rebuked systemic oppression.

While Jesus was doing the work of ministry, He was fully God and fully man. This means that He had the divine attribute of omniscience—He knew who was approaching Him for a handout, who wanted to follow Him, and who was a skeptic trying to figure Him out. Jesus knew that all these types of people were present, and He had compassion for each and every one of them. This is a divine compassion that looks at the heart of the individual, that sees them as helpless, powerless, and totally unable to change their situation—and still loves them.

Jesus never withheld mercy and compassion from those in need. Since we are not omniscient and do not know everyone's story, what gives us the right to withhold compassion and mercy from anyone? Perhaps we think, *They only want a handout.* But Jesus knew who wanted a handout—and He still poured mercy on them. Perhaps we want to avoid showing compassion because a person is skeptical that Jesus is Lord. But Jesus knew who was skeptical about Him and who would never embrace Him—yet He liberally lavished them with compassion and mercy.

Mercy means seeking to meet both the spiritual and the material needs of the marginalized in our proximity. And I know that choosing to live this way—choosing to see the people around us—can be difficult. I've certainly struggled with this myself. One hot summer day, a deacon from my church and I went out to do some street evangelism. Around noon, we decided to get out of the heat in a city restaurant and then head back to the church and pray. The restaurant was closed, so we began walking back toward the church. Just then, someone yelled at me, "Hey, who you lookin' for?"

The deacon and I both turned around. The man who had called out was shirtless, wore dirty corduroy pants, and had no shoes on—but he held a large can of beer in a brown paper bag. I said that we were fine and that I hoped he had a blessed day. As we turned to walk back toward the church, he yelled out again and began running toward us.

He approached us, out of breath, and asked if we were looking for a specific person. He then said, "That person now deals out of the back of the building," which was his way of telling us that if we wanted to buy drugs, the dealer had moved the purchase spot. I told him that we were not looking to buy drugs but that we were hungry and wanted a burrito—and that we were outside trying to share the Good News of Christ with anyone who would listen.

The man immediately became intrigued, so I asked him what he thought about God. He said immediately that he had accepted God and was doing well in life. "I appreciate your honesty," I told him. "Would you mind sharing the gospel with me?"

His expression immediately changed. "What is the gospel?" he asked. I walked him through the Good News and saw the Lord working before my eyes. The man begin weeping as I talked about the damaging effects of sin and how Jesus' work alone addressed it perfectly for us.

The man told us that he was on parole after serving five years for breaking and entering. It had been his second offense. He was fifty-three years old, couldn't find a job, had no home, and was sleeping on his mother's couch so that he could give his parole officer a legit address. Shortly after his release, he had been diagnosed with stage 4 pancreatic cancer. Every day when he woke up, he asked God the same question: "If I am right with you, give me a sign and let me know before I die—but if I am not right with you, send somebody to let me know how I can become right with you."

Then he said to us, "Today God has answered my prayer. I realize that I am not right with Him, but you have told me that there is a way to be right with Him."

I was in utter shock. God was working in real time in this man's life. Then the man asked—and I quote—"What must I do to be saved?" Both the deacon and I began weeping, and we walked him through a profession of faith in Jesus.

The very first time that this man had hollered out at us, I was more focused on getting out of the heat and back to the church. My presupposition was that he was drunk and not worthy of compassion, let alone a conversation. But Jesus wanted to meet this man, and He saved him not because of me but in spite of me.

Even when our hearts are not willing, God's sovereignty will not be stifled. Imagine if we began every morning by crucifying our flesh (Galatians 5:24) and making our hearts available to be used by God. Imagine the people living in the margins of society whose lives God will intersect with our lives. Imagine how massive social and spiritual transformation could take place if the church were to live without presupposition and with intentional compassion for the people in their proximity. This is Jesus-centered mercy, and it's what a hope-filled, reconciled people are called to share!

MARGINALIZED AUDIENCE (MATTHEW 9:35)

Tangible repentance also requires us to examine how we engage with the marginalized audience around us. Ignoring a marginalized audience means that the church will have a marginalized awareness of their existence and needs. A Jesus-centered understanding of mercy fuels Christians to run to people in their time of affliction.

It is very hard for a local church to meet the needs of people they have never met. Demographic studies can help a local church understand who their neighbors are, but those studies can't keep up with the rapid rate of transition in our communities. The church must get out and become visible to meet their neighbors. The local church should be learners of their local context. The best way to learn about a local community is by being among its residents the same way that Jesus was.

In Matthew 9:35, Jesus was traveling throughout all the cities and villages. Aside from the times when Jesus retreated to be alone with the Father and the times of personal instruction with His disciples, He was always around other people. I believe that God desires us to do the same—for those whom He has saved to be visible and engaged with those in the community who still need Jesus. There's a balance here that we must master: We as Christians should be seen doing ministry but not doing ministry to be seen. Jesus began His ministry by going to where people were, but soon, people began seeking Jesus. His availability was the magnet that attracted people, but His authenticity kept His true followers connected to Him.

The month before my family and I relocated to Atlanta, I preached four Sundays in a row at the church I was pastoring. On each of those four Sundays, I was approached by a different drug dealer. After every sermon, one of them wanted to talk to me about their need for Jesus. I invited them to go to the church library with me so that we could further discuss Jesus' call to faith and repentance. During the third conversation, with the third drug dealer, on that third Sunday, I finally had to ask—why had he approached me?

He said that drug dealers from the previous two

weeks had told him about a pastor who communicated God's truth in ways people from the street could understand. They'd said this pastor knew how to connect sinners to Jesus. My jaw dropped, and tears began to flow. The young man looked at me and said he knew the life transformation he desired would be impossible unless he first embraced Jesus. I walked him through the truth of the gospel, and he made a profession of faith. After this conversation, I challenged him to dispose of the drugs that he was going to sell. The young man said he would—which meant his supplier would be coming after him. He asked me to pray for God's protection over him. He had been selling drugs for so long and knew too much; leaving this line of work would be an immediate death sentence. That was also a motivation for embracing Jesus—he knew death could be around the corner. I invested the next few weeks in researching job leads and housing arrangements for some of the former drug dealers in need.

A note of caution: As we engage with people in the margins, we must set healthy boundaries with our availability; otherwise, we will extend ourselves too far, ruining other relationships and burning out. Jesus was fully God and fully human, so His capacity in reaching out to others was greater than ours. Every believer must wrestle with finding balance and understanding their limitations in being available to another human being. For unmarried Christians, be secure in the fact that you have the same amount of time as Christians who are married or have children. Please do not believe the lie that you have more time in a day because you're not married. The relationships you build should be meaningful and should operate within the framework of holiness as seen in Scripture. When you leverage your God-given abilities, gifts, and passions for the benefit of those with whom you are in purposeful or discipleship relationships, you will flourish.

If you are married, remember to minister to your spouse first, and to your children, if you have any. You will deal with the tension of ministering to your family and to others outside your home so that your family does not become your idol and distract you from the ministry God has given you: to build relationships with others. This is the balance: Don't sacrifice your family on the altar of ministry, but also don't neglect fellowship with and ministry to others because of family time. You will be able to discern this balance when you spend time alone with God, hearing from Him and being led by the Holy Spirit, in addition to having ongoing conversations with your family about God's leading.

The gospel Jesus preached announced the coming Kingdom, which included God's visible and tangible reach to people in the margins of society (Luke 4:16-30). Jesus has given us today His authority not only to preach the gospel of the Kingdom, which is the whole story of God, but also to make disciples from people of every imaginable ethnicity. This will mean stepping into the margins, just as Jesus did.

If we do not actively pursue people who are living in the margins of society, then we can easily remain aloof to their existence and will have marginalized awareness not only of their existence but also of Jesus' practice of distributing mercy. We must be in the habit of pursuing those who live in the margins to show them that God has not forsaken them.

MARGINALIZED INTERCESSION (MATTHEW 9:37-38)

Cultivating a heart of repentance and reconciliation means cultivating a heart of prayer. Jesus knew that His followers would struggle and desperately needed prayer—"The harvest is plentiful, but the laborers are few," He told them. The need to reach the masses living in the margins in Jesus' day was great, and Jesus knew His time on earth was ending soon. So He told His disciples to pray.

The reason Jesus challenged His disciples to pray earnestly for more laborers was so that we would depend on the movement of God and not on our own methods. The word Matthew used for "earnestly" in Matthew 9:38 means to beg and plead.[9] When my three children want something, they will not stop asking for it, even if it's as simple as going outside to play, turning on the video-game system, or ordering pizza for dinner. When they want something badly enough, they consistently beg for it. If we as God's children are not begging God for more workers to reach the harvest field, perhaps we are too comfortable in our lives and not engaged enough in reaching the people in our community. Perhaps we should seek God more and ask Him to give us unceasing grief for the marginalized of our community. This includes those who are Jesus followers and those who are not. Not every person who is homeless, an immigrant, orphaned, or widowed is a nonbeliever. We must reimagine what ministry looks like to marginalized believers in our area of proximity as well. We must not marginalize our ministry of mercy.

I've had to pray for God to make me uncomfortable on numerous occasions because it's easy for me to live off of past evangelistic success stories. It's easy for me to sit back and count how many people I have discipled or ordained into ministry. It's easy for me to sit back and count how many invitations I have received to preach—and amid resting in past or present successes, I lose hunger for those living in my own proximity. In these moments, the Lord calls me to a genuine fast from food so He can focus my heart on hungering for His work (Isaiah 58). As I seek after Him, I ask to become a burden taker rather than a burden maker for those in my community. This includes those in my own home; my next-door neighbors and those who live on my street; and the people at my grocery store, at my favorite burger stand, and in our local church.

Why is it so important to pray in this way? Matthew's words about God sending out laborers—"therefore *pray earnestly* to the Lord of the harvest to send out laborers into his harvest"—communicate that it is done without force: Praying earnestly involves passionate energy but not brute strength (Matthew 9:38, emphasis added). Sending out laborers is like releasing someone who has been waiting and preparing, like a relief pitcher in a baseball game.

When my family and I go to a Dodgers game, we love when Kenley Jansen begins his journey to the mound. Jansen is the Dodgers closer, and they bring him in to secure the lead or to stabilize the tie so that the Dodgers can either march on to victory or earn it at their next at bat. Typically, at the beginning of the ninth inning, the bullpen doors open, the Dr. Dre and Tupac classic song "California Love" comes on, and the entire stadium erupts! Here comes Jansen, jogging to the mound and ready to work.

Nobody forced Jansen out of the bullpen. Nobody held a gun to his head and told him he needed to get out there and work. Before he was called to enter the game, he was in the bullpen, warming up, anticipating the call and the open door. When it came, Jansen was not shocked or surprised. He was ready.

Jesus is calling us to be the same way. As we pray and beg for God to send laborers to reach people in the margins of society, we are called to prepare as well. Our preparation is living life together in committed relationships with those in our local church, seeking to make disciples where we live, sharing the gospel, and leveraging our life for the glory of God. We must begin each day by asking God to use us in the way that He most desires. Then, when God has prepared our hearts, He will call us to go wherever He leads. We could be the answer to somebody's prayer for Him to send laborers to the harvest field of their neighborhood—not just in the United States but also throughout the entire world.

The harvest field belongs to God, and He has given each of His followers the privilege of working in it. There is no guarantee that the work will be done in our lifetime. As a hope-filled people, we must keep the long game in mind as we see the massive amounts of work needed for equity, evangelism, and justice in our communities. We are investing in future generations, not just reaching our own. This is the reason why I have esperanza about the work of ethnic conciliation: It will continue after our generation has passed. Generation Z and all future generations will take up the mantle. This is the discipleship cycle Paul challenged Timothy to live (2 Timothy 2:2) and what he had in mind for Christian generations. When we do not marginalize our intercession, we will not marginalize our impact. Jesus-centered mercy ministry remains rooted in prayer.

REPARATIONS OF MERCY

Moving into the margins to seek forgiveness and work toward conciliation will require sacrifice—of our money, pride, and time. But consider how the church would show what the Kingdom of God is really like if we lived out this kind of sacrificial repentance for the ways we have contributed to the pain of other ethnicities. What if each of us, as we looked for places and ways we are connected to systemic sins, stood up and mobilized to make things right? Our sisters at Truth's Table have insightful contributions regarding nuances of this topic.[10]

If people who are part of denominations and networks started a movement like this that spread throughout the American Protestant church, it would go viral. This magnitude of humility in God's people as they seek the forgiveness of families they sinned against would be unprecedented in the history of humanity. And we would be meeting the needs of the afflicted while they're suffering, just like James said (James 1:26-27). Perhaps this movement could lead to a revival unlike our nation has ever seen before—where the descendants of those from Asia, indigenous nations, European countries, and Mesoamerican and African civilizations hear and see the gospel, embrace Christ, extend forgiveness, seek healing for the wounded, meet the needs of the afflicted, and live out Jesus' mission together. This movement can exist, as long as comfort and greed no longer prevent it. This is how the people of God can lead our world into ethnic conciliation.

CHAPTER 7

HOW SHOULD THE CHURCH RESPOND?

Mobilizing Transformation

"Damon, what is it going to take to see legit transformation in the communities in our country?"

This was what Elicia asked me in the wake of our time in Ferguson. As we wrestled with pain and fear and hopelessness, we were weighed down by the monumental task before the church. I'd told her I felt that the leadership in the local church needed to reflect its local community—not just ethnically but also generationally and socioeconomically. If those pursuing Jesus' mission created this sort of culture, over the course of time, the community at large would see the hope it provides. But I had no idea how we were going to get there. And so I took these questions before the throne of God.

Those hours of prayer were filled with every emotion I had ever felt in my being. I desperately cried out for clarity and insight. I needed God to give me hope because I was scared that my heart would be consumed by hate.

Slowly, the Lord began to share with me His answer: He was calling me to help the Kingdom of God become more visible through the local church. If we are ever going to be healed and whole, our communities need Jesus-centered, multiethnic, multicultural, and multigenerational-led churches modeling long-lasting engagement, intersecting the six avenues of life with the gospel, and mobilizing others to do the same.

- **Jesus-centered.** Jesus is the central figure in God's story, and the gospel is the bridge that connects God's story to our story. A robust gospel that focuses on all of Jesus' work should be the lens through which those in the local church view the world. The gospel enables us to see all humans as equal image bearers of God. We have all inherited a sinful nature from Adam (Romans 5:12) and are all in equal need of the Savior, Jesus Christ (John 14:6), who is working to make all things new (Revelation 21:5). This robust gospel should be central in our discipleship as God the Holy Spirit daily transforms every area of our lives, not just our theology, as we live together in community.

- **Multiethnic, multicultural, and multigenerational-led.** The local church should diligently work to ensure its leadership reflects the ethnic, generational, and socioeconomic demographics of its area. This will provide on-ramps for conversations with members of the community who sense they have legit representation in leaders who understand their nuances. The leaders should all be biblically qualified (1 Timothy 3:1-7; Titus 1:6-16) and strive to ensure stable health in the pulpit, people, and processes of the church. These leaders are focused on not only shepherding the hearts of their people but also raising up like-minded future leaders (2 Timothy 2:2). The idea is for the leaders to be indigenous to the community where the church is located.

- **Model long-lasting engagement.** Church leaders should work with the Lord's leading to take root in the community God has called them to. Each leader should desire to remain there for as long as God allows. Success is not measured by numerical or monetary growth but rather by being faithful to the Scriptures, equipping the next generations with a proper understanding of God's story, and seeing spiritual maturity becoming the new rhythm of life in the community at large, not just inside the church building. This kind of intentional investment takes decades, not months.

- **Intersect the six avenues of life with the gospel.** The gospel should be faithfully and strategically woven into the **FABRIC** of community life.

  Family—The Christian home is the first mission field, and those within the local church should model and multiply a Jesus-centered emphasis that mirrors Ephesians 5:22–6:4, Colossians 3:18–4:1, and 1 Peter 3:1-7. Since the church is God's family, our understanding of family should include nuance and space for blended families, unmarried believers,[1] and foster care and adoptive members. All of these voices have value; none are second-class citizens in the Kingdom.

  Authority (Scripture, government, and law enforcement)—We must model what it looks like to pray for our national, state, and local leaders (1 Timothy 2:1-6). Additionally, we must couple our prayers with a lifestyle of submission to the authority of God's Word first and our government authorities second (Romans 13:1-7; 1 Peter 2:13-17). Yet we must also consider the call to speak out against injustice and mobilize to do justice on both spiritual and social levels in our community.

Business—We must consider how our finances will help those in need (Philippians 4:10-20) and flourish the communities we worship in. We must show store owners in our neighborhood that God's people practice generosity and contentment (1 Timothy 6:6-10). All the while, we must seek to help the unemployed find employment, even if that means creating job opportunities for them.

Religion—We must ask Jesus to fill our hearts with His compassion (Matthew 9:35-38) as we reasonably respond to those who oppose our faith (1 Peter 3:13-17). We must diligently discover how to translate God's story to people groups living in our proximity and reach out to them as we make Christ known. In addition, we must offer apologetic insights to counter the ethnocentric cults that proselytize Christians of non-European descent who struggle with not having their ethnicity affirmed.

Institutions (education, elder care, and rehabilitation)—We must invest time in securing employment and in volunteering in local schools, retirement homes, hospice centers, jails, and prisons. We must also lobby for education and prison reform to enter our community; we must respond to the cries of our city that resemble Psalm 10:10-18.

Culture (arts and entertainment)—We must view the culture through the lens of God's story before we engage it. We must examine the culture's belief system, language, and practices in light of Scripture so we can find ways to relate while remaining morally pure. Our speech should be filled with hope and concepts the culture can understand so that we can build relationships with the people around us. We will fight against sinning to gain approval (Acts 17:16-34). The relationships we develop will be in harmony with Paul's method in 1 Thessalonians 2:8.

- **Mobilize others to do the same.** As church leaders live out the above nuances, they'll organically launch their people to daily do the same.

The vision God embedded in my heart that day, alongside the mosaic montage of Generation Z, fuels my heart with hope for the future of the American Protestant church. I genuinely believe we're on the cusp of seeing the gospel's power in full display, evidenced by the ethnic, generational, and socioeconomic diversity in Christ's body becoming more visible every day. We in the church can display the Kingdom by communicating God's message of ethnic conciliation, establishing key relationships for the work, and raising up local leaders. Our future is esperanza.

The big picture for the local church is to know how they can minister to all people by serving them as agents of the shalom God has made available through Jesus. Through the incarnational work of Jesus, He provides the pathway to shalom (Ephesians 2:11-22). So the incarnational body of Christ (the church) should apply a balanced approach for human flourishing in their communities. Here's what I mean by **HUMAN**:

- *Habitat* (social spaces)—addressing issues working against flourishing in the home, church, community, city, nation, and world.

- *Understanding* (intellect)—learning and processing history, the present, and the projected future righteously.

- *Material* (physical bodies)—acknowledging and striving to meet dietary needs, clothing, exercise, employment opportunities, fair wages, hygiene, righteous sexual expression, and affordable housing for self and others.

- *Affection* (emotions)—developing healthy pathways of becoming aware, coping, expressing, and healing in the areas of emotions, mental illnesses, stress factors, and abuse (emotional, physical, sexual, spiritual, substance, and verbal).

- *Non-Material* (spiritual)—recognizing the God-given soul that every image bearer has received and sharing the Good News that Jesus as the only qualified Savior who redeems.

Since Jesus is the shalom of all His followers and because He's created the pathway to peace both vertically (with God) and horizontally (with the body), the whole church can be agents of shalom by engaging in the work of **HUMAN** flourishing.

A RAPID RESPONSE

When we begin and continue the work of ethnic conciliation, we may be labeled too liberal for conservatives and too conservative for liberals. The pain often felt in the cross fire from being attacked by both sides is real. As we endure this suffering together, God will meld our hearts together. Through our local churches, we'll be able to press on, more unified in showing our communities that King Jesus is concerned with such issues as:

- *Women's Rights.* We must fight for women to be esteemed as equal image bearers with men and not sex objects. We should advocate for fair work wages and access to education for women, and we should seek to platform their voices because Jesus demonstrated that they have value although our society says they don't (Luke 10:39-42; 13:16; and John 4:1-42).

- *Immigration/Refugees.* Every human is an image bearer, and societies are built on the family unit. We must fight to reunite families that have been separated. We should protect vulnerable women and children and lobby for policy reform that helps those seeking asylum and provides them with pathways to citizenship.

- *Economic Equity.* We should diligently work to help create jobs for those living in the margins of our society and help them earn fair wages. We should invest resources that can open opportunities for creative entrepreneur ventures, provide assistance for the homeless, and create reentry programs.

- *Education Reform.* The high-risk students in our cities must have access to tutors, nourishing lunches, and quality education. They should be assisted in finding financial aid for post-secondary-education opportunities and, at minimum, see God's people love them through faithful volunteerism.

- *Religious Liberty.* We should speak out against all religious persecution. We should depend on the power of God found through prayer and faithful study of God's Word, and we should not place our hope in the government alone.

- *The Sanctity of Life.* We must believe and preach that every life is precious, not just the ones forming in their mother's womb but also those who need care after they are born and until they are laid to rest with a dignified burial.[2]

The gospel Jesus preached consists of balancing His salvific atoning work and social action with the non-believing world. It is this same gospel that addresses the sin of partiality that's been embraced and unchecked in America for far too long. If we seek to live out the full gospel, the local church must diligently work to provide its local community with a **RAPID** response to every area touching ethnic conciliation. This means our work should be to:

- *Restore* dignity to every image bearer by helping meet their HUMAN needs
- *Affirm* the ethnic identity of every Jesus follower (fellow Kingdom citizens)
- *Promote* the Kingdom ethics Jesus commands us to practice socially and spiritually

- *Institute* the work of ethnic conciliation and weave the gospel into the FABRIC of your community
- *Develop* biblical guardrails for limited engagement with nonbelievers as cobelligerents

THREE KEY RELATIONSHIPS

I believe local churches engaged in the work of ethnic conciliation need to establish three types of relationships to represent the Kingdom of God and accomplish human flourishing in their community: colaborers, compadres, and cobelligerents.

Colaborers

These are churches and parachurch organizations that align philosophically and theologically on all primary and most secondary issues. These may be churches within our denomination or network structures. Working with colaborers is the easiest and most comfortable of the three relationships, which is why the other two types of relationships are necessary.

Compadres

In Spanish, the term *compadre* has two meanings. First, it refers to a child's godfather. According to the Roman Catholic tradition in my family, the compadre is a trusted family member or friend who stands with the parents at the baby's christening and assumes responsibility for the child if the parents can no longer care for the baby. The second meaning of compadre is *friend*. Churches, especially church plants, should seek out compadres, developing strong partnerships with other local churches that are firm on the essentials of the Christian faith but may differ in opinion on secondary issues. The younger church will gain credibility in the community when it seeks an older, established local church to walk alongside. This partnership communicates that the younger church does not think they've been sent by Jesus to replace an old and unsuccessful church; rather, by working to support the older church, the younger church shows that Jesus has called them to join Him on His mission in the community. For this to happen, evangelicals will need to branch out beyond their tribe and build relationships with mainline churches that share a common understanding of the gospel and Jesus' mission.

Cobelligerents

Francis Schaeffer popularized the idea of cobelligerence and often received pushback for his views on it. *Cobelligerence* is when two enemies unite to fight against a common enemy. The question Jesus' church must ask is: *When is it proper to partner with nonbelievers to address a common social ill in our community?* Schaeffer said,

Christians must realize that there is a difference between being a cobelligerent and an ally. At times we will seem to be saying exactly the same thing as those without a Christian base are saying. If there is social injustice, say there is social injustice. If we need order, say we need order. In these cases, and at these specific points, we would be cobelligerents. But we must not align ourselves as though we are in any camp built on a non-Christian base. We are an ally of no such camp. The church of the Lord Jesus Christ is different—totally different. . . .

We must say what the Bible says when it causes us *to seem to be saying* what others are saying, such as "Justice!" or "Stop the meaningless bombings!" But we must never forget that this is only a passing cobelligerency and not an alliance.[3]

Schaeffer qualified his thoughts in an interview with Martin Wroe and Dave Roberts: "I have two words which I would recommend to anybody . . . and they are 'ally' and 'co-belligerent.' An ally is a person who is a born-again Christian with whom I can go a long way down the road. . . . A co-belligerent is a person who may not have any sufficient basis for taking the right position but takes the right position on a single issue."[4] According to Schaeffer, Christians can and should engage with nonbelievers on a short-term basis when they agree on a single issue. Cobelligerence can help address a social ill or event if approached with a biblical framework and a clear timeline for the church's engagement alongside the nonbelieving entity. Here is how you might be **ABLE** to employ such a framework:

- *Apply Wisdom* (Matthew 10:16): Be evangelistic during the time of interaction. But don't be overly romantic. Expect some hostility because the convictions of those you're alongside may not be rooted in or in pursuit of Jesus.

- *Be Clear* (2 Corinthians 6:14-18): Realize that your mission is to represent God's Kingdom and live out Kingdom ethics. Jesus' church transcends the social ills you're addressing. Remember, the gospel's power does not rise or fall because of partnership with any movement. So clearly communicate short-term participation in cobelligerency, and make sure you continue gospel-saturated work in your community after these events are over, without partnering with the cobelligerents, to safeguard your biblical convictions and the distinction of the church's mission.

- *Live Pure* (Ephesians 5:1-14): Abstain from any sinful activities that those in your cobelligerency practice. If, while joining them in lobbying or protest, you decide to participate in acts of hate, sensuality, or other forms of sin, you're no longer distinct in morality or mission and must confess (1 John 1:8-10), repent (2 Corinthians 7:9-11), and seek restoration (Galatians 6:1-2).

- *Engage Responsibly* (James 1:22-27): Be committed in ministering to the widows, orphans, and poor in your city that are part of the systemic oppression. Evangelicals in your city may have often neglected these people before, and your commitment will show cobelligerents your long-term priorities.

RAISING UP LOCAL LEADERS

If we look at the book of Revelation, we discover an incredible truth: Our ethnicity remains with us throughout eternity (Revelation 7:9). This is by God's design. When we affirm ethnic heritage, we give God glory and guard against falling into idolatry or partiality. We can find a balance in affirming others' ethnicities when we build interethnic relationships with our brothers and sisters in Christ. We must realize that we can't build relationships until we're willing to enter into the worlds of those who are different from us.

I entered into evangelical Christian higher academia

to build such relationships because evangelical Christian higher academia was not pursuing my world or me. I patiently endured forced assimilation to gain trust, so my outsider perspective could be heard. In God's grace, the relationships I've built (with my fathers in the faith) have enriched my walk with Christ, and now I am a cultural hybrid with a personal mission to network my two worlds: the nongentrified parts of my city and evangelicalism.

I pray that individually and institutionally, the American church can dissolve the dichotomy between these two worlds. But the mission will not be accomplished until we stop seeing contextualization without representation. Here's what I mean by that: Often, we attempt to contextualize the gospel's message and method in our cities today, but we do not raise up people from the target demographic in equal leadership as we contextualize. The indigenous urbanite is a diamond in the rough. At first glance, people in these contexts may look like coal, but the pressures of living where other people fled from decades ago have developed them into diamonds. Three considerations must take place for their excavation: (1) we must consider their context; (2) we must work through challenges in locating them; and (3) we must advocate for and act toward systemic changes inside Protestant church-leadership structures.

Context

In the United States, more than 80 percent of the population lives in urban areas.[5] The "browning of America" is our reality because ethnic minority populations have the highest population increases in urban settings.[6] *USA Today* reported that in 2011, for the first time in America's history, the majority of all babies born—50.4 percent—were minorities.[7] We're closing in on ten years of this turning of the tides, and this trend has not stopped.

Gentrification is taking place in areas that were already brown before condos, Whole Foods, and hot yoga spots opened up. Community gatekeepers who are of non-European descent have lived there, raised kids, and remained in the areas as empty nesters. If we in the church want to identify persons of peace or bridge builders, those who have long lived in the target area can best provide valuable perspectives on the rhythm of life in the community.

Church leaders and other Christians who have been called by God to transplant into communities in transition should do so with humility. They should genuinely make it a priority to love their neighbors and listen to legacy leaders in the area—especially if their neighbors and local leaders are of different ethnicities than their own.

Parachuting in with an arrogant heart and a savior mentality will be counterproductive from the very beginning. I should know—I did this the first time I planted a church. Although I was born and raised in Kansas City, Kansas, I chose to plant a church where Elicia grew up, across the river in the Historic Northeast area of Kansas City, Missouri. Although the cities share the same name, the rhythm of life between the neighborhoods Elicia and I were raised in is like night and day. Her neighborhood was like a second neighborhood to me, but I planted a church in it not realizing the ways my heart was set against the community and, more specifically, the churches that were already present.

Recently, I went back to look at my original church-planting strategy and the first few sermons I preached. I regularly criticized other churches, expressing how they had been ineffective for decades. I painted a bleak, grim picture of the community's issues—the drug game, gang warfare, prostitution, and violent crime—saying that rampant sin was due to ministry failures of each of the sixty churches within the one-mile radius of our meeting location. Back then, I didn't realize my arrogance, but now, it's all I can see. It was as if I low-key believed that God had specifically selected me to be His representative to save the community and the people in it from destruction. Thankfully, through almost six years of pastoring precious souls and by God's mercy and grace, I was able to confess my arrogance and repent of it.

By the time the Lord called Elicia and me to plant a church in Long Beach, I had long repented of this high level of arrogance and moved with a greater awareness that I must go into the community as a learner first. I communicated publicly and privately that God was calling my family and others to join in Jesus' mission *alongside* the faithful saints who had been there for decades before our arrival.

We sought to develop thriving friendships and partnerships with other pastors and churches. Our strategy—and hope—was that within the first few years, most of the church leadership would be natives of Los Angeles. We prayed that the demographics of the congregation and leadership would reflect the demographics of the city of Long Beach. But raising up this type of Kingdom leadership would require us to identify and work through a few issues.

Challenges

The challenges we face in developing Kingdom leaders of all ethnicities can vary based on our context and our individual call, but in this work of ethnic conciliation, we experience some similar battles. When we planted our church in Long Beach, the key challenges I encountered spoke directly to the heart of ethnic conciliation.

One challenge was that I needed to focus on planting a church for the demographic God called me to instead of trying to plant the church of my dreams. This is often true for church leaders who are called to transplant into churches that have plateaued or are dying. These leaders may need to understand the nations that God has brought into their neighborhood and seek, through evangelism and discipleship, to produce Kingdom fruit so the community on the outside sees representation inside the church.

Another challenge I faced was the need to identify potential leaders. I'm a firm believer that Jesus gives gifts to His church (Ephesians 4:8): the people that He saves. This means that every man, woman, and child who the Holy Spirit regenerates and brings into fellowship in the local church is a gift directly from Jesus to that body. According to Ephesians 4:11-16, church leaders, who are also Jesus' gifts, are to equip church members to do the work of ministry so that the whole body can mature.

The gifts Jesus sent to our church plants in both Kansas City and Long Beach were answers to the prayers of myself and other leaders. We prayed specifically for God to send persons of peace to become part of our fellowship. A person of peace is someone from the local community who joins and helps serve in the new or revitalizing church. The person of peace brings a credibility that the transplanting Christian does not. The person of peace also can serve the local church leaders by providing them with clear insight on cultural lifestyles and expected and taboo practices that the church must be mindful of.

In some situations, the Lord may provide inroads with a person of peace through the work of evangelism. In this case, church leaders and members must identify the social spaces in which the people of the community enjoy doing life. This is what Ray Oldenburg calls the "third place" in his book *The Great Good Place*. If the first place in which a person spends their time is home, and their second place is work, then the third place is where they go voluntarily and regularly.[8] For some people, this third place may be the barber shop or the golf course, and for others, it may be the basketball court or a bomb taco truck. Wherever the people in your community frequent is the third place that you must integrate into your life rhythm.

For me, a local park in Long Beach has provided opportunities to develop relationships that started with casual conversations and eventually allowed me to ask how I could pray for that person. Exchanging phone numbers with a couple of men I have met there has given me the opportunity to text them encouraging words and build rapport. A few months into some of the relationships, the individuals would reach out to me and initiate ways that I could pray for them and help their families in times of need. The fact that I would respond and engage with them provided greater spaces for me to share the love of God and the gospel with them.

In other situations, the Lord may send believers of

different ethnicities who are persons of peace in the community directly to the new or revitalizing church. These persons of peace are looking for discipleship relationships as well as guidance on how to reach the community they were born and raised in. This is where honest conversations must take place. Sometimes it takes a while for the indigenous Christians to see the transplants who moved to their city develop a legit love for the people of their city. This can cause walls of self-preservation to be built early in the ministry's life. The best way to proactively lay strong foundations for long-lasting and meaningful relationships is to have indigenous Christians express their fears and ask questions about the mission and vision of the new or revitalizing church and for transplanting Christians to answer with authenticity.

When a pipeline for leadership is developed, and indigenous leaders are placed in it, a final challenge emerges. This challenge is to ensure that the indigenous Christian is not eye candy or a token put on display to attract others of their ethnic heritage. Whatever the dominant culture of the church might be, those of different ethnicities who are being developed as leaders need to be protected from being the spokesperson for their entire ethnicity or for other ethnic-minority people groups.

At the same time, these emerging leaders should be empowered, affirmed, and installed into the highest levels of leadership where executive decisions are made. If these people are being raised up into pastoring, current leaders must commit to provide them with regular time in the pulpit and other spaces for them to teach. The developing leaders must also be included in the process of decision making. Their counsel, experience, and wisdom can potentially help make decisions that cause flourishing rather than frustration in the church and the community. Lastly, when these leaders are given responsibility, current leaders must allow them to make mistakes and fail. An environment in which it is safe to fail is necessary for emerging leaders to grow and develop as well as for protecting the church from an elitist and paternalistic view of leadership.

These challenges may seem daunting, but they are not impossible. Current church leaders must be willing to let go of certain structures or glass ceilings that have been used to prohibit ethnic diversity in leadership. The church must be dedicated to making the necessary changes so that the Kingdom of God can be more holistically represented in leadership.

Changes

The third piece of raising up local leaders is openness to and advocacy for change. Trying to establish or revitalize a church in a transitioning community can seem romantic on paper. However, the honeymoon phase disappears quickly, and the work ahead becomes more visible. The church must be willing to change in response to the realities they face.

The biggest change a church must make is to commit to know the community in humble and contextual ways. Doing this will take a little bit of work. I like to use the illustration of double Dutch. Double Dutch involves three people. The first two people are standing across from each other, separated by the length of two jump ropes, one in each hand. As they begin swinging the ropes in opposing directions and singing, the third person begins learning the rhythm of the ropes. They observe the moving ropes so they can order their steps to the beat and not stop the flow or the rhythm of the ropes. When the third person is ready, they jump in, sing this song with the other two people, and keep the rhythm. The third person's goal is to keep their steps in sync with the rhythm of the song and the ropes. If they misstep or get off beat, the rope will hit their foot and the game will stop.

Similarly, those who are transplanting into transitioning communities should consider the two ropes their society is holding. The first rope is the anthropological history of the community: the history of the people who founded the neighborhood, served as leaders, and lived there. When they were thriving, they set trends for the community; however, their day has gone, and the community has changed. The second rope represents the sociological contemporary rhythms. This is the current population in the community and the life rhythms they are setting for the neighborhood.

As the person jumping between these two ropes, the transplanter must study the history and contemporary trends to identify the beat of the neighborhood and develop movement that is in sync. This will allow the transplanter to know when God wants them to jump in or out while remaining in step with the community. Making mistakes and poor judgment calls in church planting is inevitable (trust me, I know). But the good news is that, like when a misstep takes place in double Dutch, the game can start over if the jumper asks those holding the ropes to "run 'em back." Similarly, when the transplanter trips up, they can run 'em back by consulting locals who can help them assess the contemporary trends and begin a rhythm that is in sync with the community.

As life rhythms provide transplanters with acceptance and third places and the transplanters identify cultural hybrids who could be persons of peace, the transplanting Christian must remember that the cultural hybrids are diamonds in the rough. The transplanter is not affirming their value by discovering them; rather, these people have had value all the while and must now be allowed to step into spaces where God's radiance can be seen through their life.

Often, diamonds are rated by the four Cs: color, clarity, cut, and carat weight. The four Cs necessary for preparing diamonds in the rough for leadership are *Christ*, *compassion*, *commitment*, and *community*.

First, the diamond in the rough needs to root their identity in Jesus Christ, seeking to imitate Him. It is His social and spiritual commands they are called to obey and teach to others (Matthew 28:20). Second, these emerging leaders need believers in their lives who extend them compassion, just as Jesus did in Matthew 9:35-38. Third, these people need commitment from leaders. The leaders must carve out times where they can raise up future leaders through discipleship relationships (2 Timothy 2:2). Fourth, local leaders need to be embraced by the community within the local church and by other churches in the local community.

These quality relationships do not develop overnight. Often, leaders may start off strong and well-intentioned early in the relationship but falter over time. Current leaders who are raising up diamonds in the rough must learn to **PACE** themselves.

- *Patience*—God is patient with all His children, so all His children must be patient with each other. This means we must fight off passive aggressiveness and communicate honestly when we are frustrated, disappointed, or offended. Conflict is a litmus test for relationships. It shows the level of depth a relationship has. When conflict arises, if a relationship is shallow, allowing things to simmer under the surface can go on for an extended amount of time, preventing the relationship from going deeper. If the relationship is meaningful, the issue will be resolved and the relationship will grow deeper than before the conflict surfaced.

- *Active Listening*—This is a call to hear the developing leader's heart, not just their tone. If they lacked a father figure in their life, they may have a hard time trusting or committing to a discipleship relationship. If they had traumatic childhood experiences, they may struggle to maintain healthy relationships. Active listening is essential; the diamond in the rough must be given the opportunity to open up and vent about their heart wounds. This may be the first time in their life they've felt safe enough to take this risk. Do not abandon them after they have done this.

- *Correct* (when necessary)—Part of Jesus' design for discipleship includes teaching others to obey His spiritual and social commands. Teaching is not just transferring information but coming alongside and walking with another person who is being transformed by the same Holy Spirit. At times, behavior patterns and sin will need to be identified, called out, and corrected. Growth and maturity also need to be identified and affirmed. Both are crucial in developing the diamond in the rough.

- *Equip*—The gospel speaks not only to the theology of the believer but also to their whole being. Leaders must walk holistically with their potential leaders. They must share tools that deal with emotional intelligence, financial stewardship, mental health, sexual purity, soul care, and time management, to name a few. The more well-rounded a leader is, the better they can help meet the needs of their church and community.

In my pastoral ministry, I have been privileged to raise up pupils into peers. They entered the pupil stage when they asked me to take them under my wing and import my life into theirs as we grew in Christ together. They were then affirmed as peers when I raised them up alongside me in leadership. At this stage, I publicly affirmed them as pastors and regularly reminded people that I was one of many pastors and that when I needed pastoring, these were the men I turned to.

When ethnic diversity is established in leadership, the congregation will have a clearer definition of success. Success is not measured by the number of people attending a worship service or the number of commas in the annual budget but by the leaders who steadily remain faithful to Scripture, diligently work toward spiritual maturity becoming the culture of the church, and equip the next generation with a strong development system for the church's future. When these things take place, we will see multiethnic, multicultural, and multi-generational leadership, not only in local church communities but also in schools, conferences, interpersonal relationships, and American Protestant denominations. Here are a few questions that evangelicals can ask— corporately and individually—to see whether Kingdom diversity is being applied in their spheres of influence:

- **Denominational Structures:** How is ethnic diversity reflected in the denomination leadership with decision-making power? Do those with executive-level decision-making responsibilities all share the same ethnic heritage, gender, social class, and political affiliations? Is our executive team willing to entrust tomorrow's leaders with denominational influence today?

- **Higher-Academic Institutions:** Does the ethnic diversity in our student body reflect the ethnic demography of the city we're positioned in? Does the ethnic makeup of our faculty, staff, president's cabinet, and student body reflect the diversity of the Kingdom (Revelation 7:9)? Are our students challenged to read authors of ethnicities, genders, and theological orientations different from those of the professor?[9]

- **Conference Lineups:** Do the plenary speakers of our event reflect the demographic of the nation in which the event occurs? Are our ethnic-minority speakers only asked to speak on issues dealing with race, niche musical movements, or urban ministry? Have the direct needs of women been addressed by including women's voices and perspectives during our planning sessions?

- **Pastoral Roles:** Are the words *multicultural, multiethnic,* and *multigenerational* used to describe our congregation but not our pastoral leadership team? Is ethnic diversity present in our church's pulpit? Has the church considered the dangers of tokenism and eye candy as motivations for hiring staff of different ethnicities?

- **Interpersonal Relationships:** Have I shut down talks about ethnicity or race because I'm afraid to lose a friend? Have I asked my friends of other ethnicities if I've ever offended them with off-color jokes or comments I've made in ignorance? Am I willing to intentionally enter the homes and worlds of other believers whose ethnicities differ from mine?

THIS WORK TOGETHER

The work of ethnic conciliation should produce HUMAN flourishing as God's people work together as agents of shalom in their homes and communities. It is also a corporate reality that each of us who follow Jesus must work together to bring to life—from the grassroots level all the way up to the executive levels in our churches, denominations, and institutions of higher learning. By weaving the whole gospel into the FABRIC of our communities, we can practice a RAPID response—which allows us to be ABLE to evangelize and raise up local leaders at a Spirit-guided PACE. When we do this, we will see the Kingdom reflected in all the spaces of our lives—our church denominations and our conferences, our educational intuitions and businesses, our local churches and our homes. This is the holistic approach to ethnic conciliation.

CHAPTER 8

KINGDOM ETHICS FOR A KINGDOM ETHNICITY

Becoming a Brochure of Heaven

The 2016 election almost single-handedly took away the esperanza I held in my heart. In the months leading up to the election, I sensed a unity among evangelicals that I had never felt before. The conversation focused on the dangers of Hillary Clinton winning the election and how the church needed to rally together because our greatest days of persecution were ahead.

A few days after the election, I was asked to speak at a worldview seminar in Dallas, Texas. One of the speakers before me joked about Millennials who were crying about the election results. As I sat in that auditorium, surrounded by a few thousand high-school students, my heart sank. *You are the speaker*, I thought, *and you're making light of the suffering that people of non-European descent are enduring.* During my talk, I addressed his comments. I talked about the need for compassion instead of humor, which only furthered the pain people were experiencing.

I talked about children who were weeping in fear of their parents being deported while they were at school. About Mexicans living in border states who had "Build the wall!" shouted at them while they pumped gas. These stories were no laughing matter. These were people with names, hearts, and souls. Little did I know that in that very room were Christian high-school teachers who had spent the past few days consoling dozens of students who had experienced similar treatment from their classmates. When I stepped off the stage, a couple of teachers and a handful of students were waiting for me, tears streaming down their faces. I had spoken up for them in a room filled with people who were speaking out against them. My comments offended people in places of power, but I was not going to back down from speaking a needed prophetic word amid tension.

AMERICANS WHO ARE CHRISTIANS OR A CHRISTIAN AMERICA?

In America, we have a highly polarized and politicized society. Often, American Christians assume that our relationship to Jesus connects to how we vote. I've seen

Christians break fellowship with other Christians because of the candidate they voted for. We constantly talk *at* each other and not *to* each other. We lace our speech with binary terms—for example, telling each other that voting for a third-party candidate is actually voting for the candidate we don't like.

In the 2016 election, my fear was that the church would respond to Trump's victory like friends in my youth group did when Evander Holyfield defeated Mike Tyson. My friends interpreted that boxing match as a Christianity-versus-Muslim bout, and when Holyfield was declared victor, they assumed the church had won. After the election, my fear was realized when I heard believers speak about Trump's win as if it was Jesus' win. When I saw evangelical leaders begin to esteem Trump as if he were God's candidate, I immediately thought of something Francis Schaeffer said: "We should not wrap Christianity in our national flag."[1]

I also remembered where I was the night that Barack Obama was declared the winner of the 2008 election. Bible-college students gathered around the rec room, watching as the poll results came in, state-by-state. They echoed comments I'd heard from adult Christians— about how they couldn't see how true believers in Jesus could vote for Barack Obama. Then Obama was declared the victor—and our president-elect. I got text messages from friends who were ecstatic and filled with joy and hope for the first time in their life. And I got text messages from Christians who were concerned that the Antichrist was taking his seat in the White House and that Jesus' return was around the corner.

The next morning, I was sitting in my office when a young African American student knocked at my door. This was his first semester in a Bible-college setting. He was from a rough part of the city, and the college campus was twenty miles away from his home—culturally, light-years away. He and I had connected throughout his first few months to provide each other with some familiarity of city life. I worried he was having a hard time adjusting, although I knew he was resilient, smart, and strong.

The morning after the election was his breaking point. For the entire time he had been at Bible college— which was also election season—he had constantly heard people's fears of Obama becoming president. The night of the election, he sat among students who took out their frustration with the results on him. He simply could not bounce back from their hurtful statements, and he entered my office to tell me he was done—he was leaving the school. I didn't try to convince him to stay. All I could do was weep with him.

After our conversation, I asked him if he would accompany me to speak to the college president about what he had endured. The president met with us imme-diately; later that day, he rebuked the treatment the young man had endured and expressed a zero-tolerance policy for such abuse. The young man refused to identify the offending students and said he already forgave them. He left the school, and we still stay connected. He's doing well as a solid preacher of God's Word, but the treatment he received breaks my heart to this day. The politicization of faith is not in step with the Kingdom ethics of God's people, because we are all part of one new Kingdom ethnicity (Ephesians 2:11-22).

WE ARE EXILES

The Kingdom ethics we should strive to live out as Jesus followers are throughout the Sermon on the Mount. And we shouldn't just listen to Jesus' words—we must make the conscious decision to put feet to our faith and walk them out. It is crucial, therefore, to bring the words of James into dialogue with the Sermon on the Mount. We become poor in spirit when we declare spiritual bankruptcy, recognizing that we need Jesus' shed blood to remove our sin debt. And as Jesus tells us, the poor in spirit are citizens of God's Kingdom (Matthew 5:3). We have been born again (John 3:3-8), we are new creations (2 Corinthians 5:17), and the Holy Spirit indwells us, transforming our whole life (Romans 8:9-13; 12:1-21).

These are beautiful truths, but they will remain only a theory inside our theological textbooks if we reduce them to conversations divorced from our lifestyle. This is why the book of James is important. James provided counsel to the fathers and mothers of our faith, who were living in the margins of a society that saw them as insignificant. James calls every follower of Jesus to examine their personal comforts and prejudices. He tells them to examine the words they use and discern how to respond during times of suffering and trial they encounter. The people James was writing to were aliens in a foreign land, sojourners from a distant kingdom, traveling through a country that was not their home.

In America, both our society and our churches have power structures, practices, and prejudices that restrict the gospel's work. Just as he wrote to the early Christians, James is calling us to unshackle ourselves from such structures to find the freedom Jesus gives us. We can root our identity not in where we live or where we were born but in God's Kingdom, which transcends every country, culture, and comfort.

THE WAYS OF THE KINGDOM

In America today, Christians are divided on how to define the gospel. In evangelicalism, leaders express the central gospel message (in content) but neglect to apply this message to the social turmoil surrounding them (in context).[2]

On the other hand, those in mainline Christianity

see the church's mission as mobilizing social action to alleviate injustice, representing the Kingdom of God, and loving our neighbors—while forsaking the message of Christ's atoning work.[3]

But we miss the full gospel if we choose one side over the other. Our behavior as Christians is an outward expression of what we believe, and what we believe should trace back to the words of King Jesus. Our lifestyle should line up under Jesus' lordship, both socially and spiritually. Jesus tells His disciples to "make disciples of all nations" and "[teach] them to observe all that I have commanded you" (Matthew 28:19-20). And so, in our Kingdom ethnicity, the social and spiritual commands of Jesus should inform everything we do.

In His teachings, Jesus gives His followers commands that are to be obeyed in real time through our lips and our lifestyle. Here are a few examples of the social commands of Jesus:

- Practice human flourishing. (Matthew 5:3-12)
- Let your light shine. (Matthew 5:14-16)
- Proclaim God's law and Jesus' fulfillment of the law. (Matthew 5:17)
- Reconcile your strained relationships. (Matthew 5:23-25)
- Stop lusting. (Matthew 5:27-28)
- Stop lying. (Matthew 5:37)

- Serve your oppressor. (Matthew 5:38-42)
- Love your enemies. (Matthew 5:44-46)
- Be perfect. (Matthew 5:46-48)
- Seek God's Kingdom first. (Matthew 6:19-21)
- Do not judge wrongfully, but make discerning decisions. (Matthew 7:1-3)
- Live the Golden Rule. (Matthew 7:12)
- Walk the narrow and unpopular path. (Matthew 7:13-14)
- Protect and value children. (Matthew 18:10)
- Confront sinning Christians and restore them in love. (Matthew 18:15-17)
- Honor marriage as God defines it. (Matthew 19:4-6)
- Always serve the poor. (Luke 14:12-14)
- Pay your taxes. (Matthew 22:19-21)
- Make disciples. (Matthew 28:19-20)

In addition to these social commands, Jesus calls us to obey His spiritual commands:

- Repent. (Matthew 4:17)
- Follow Jesus only. (Matthew 4:19)
- Store up treasures that are eternal. (Matthew 6:19-21)
- Never stop praying. (Matthew 7:7-8)
- Know and listen to God's voice. (Matthew 11:15)

- Love God and your neighbors holistically. (Matthew 22:37-40)
- Become born again. (John 3:3-8)
- Keep His commandments. (John 14:15)

When we make these social and spiritual commands of Jesus the framework of our lifestyles, we show the distinction between God's people and the people of the world. In Luke 24:46-49, Jesus said that His suffering, death, and resurrection occurred so that His followers could proclaim repentance and the forgiveness of sins to every ethnicity. His followers were to begin in Jerusalem, where they were geographically located, and they were to wait in that city until they were given power from on high. The power from the Holy Spirit would give them the boldness to make Jesus known in Jerusalem, Judea, Samaria, and throughout the entire world (Acts 1:8).

After the coming of the Holy Spirit (Acts 2), the church became mobile because of persecution (Acts 8). Throughout Scripture, we see that God does not want His people to remain stuck in the false idea that this earth is their final home. God's people are *sojourners* walking with God (Psalm 39:12), *citizens of heaven* (Philippians 3:20), *sojourners and exiles* (1 Peter 2:11), and *strangers and exiles on the earth* who are looking toward the heavenly City of God (Hebrews 11:13-16).

Americans are not exempt from these truths. There

is nothing wrong with being grateful for and respecting the country of our birth; however, there is a difference between appreciating the country you live in and idolizing it. When we wrap the Christian faith in the flag of our country, we have added a foreign ingredient to our faith. This is syncretism. When we do this, we must repent and let go of this form of idolatry. Let us cling only to the cross of Christ, which stands above the Statue of Liberty.

Although Lady Liberty says, "Give me your tired, your poor, your huddled masses yearning to breathe free," the marginalized in our nation feel she and her systems have rejected them. Yet it was Jesus who said first, "Come to me, all who labor and are heavy laden, and I will give you rest. Take my yoke upon you, and learn from me, for I am gentle and lowly in heart, and you will find rest for your souls. For my yoke is easy, and my burden is light" (Matthew 11:28-30). Jesus also said, "All that the Father gives me will come to me, and whoever comes to me I will never cast out" (John 6:37). Our King Jesus not only has an open invitation for people from every nation, tribe, and tongue to come to Him but also guarantees that He will never turn away anyone whom the Father draws to Him!

Every broken soul who comes to Jesus feels His healing embrace and is welcomed into His Kingdom. The Kingdom of Jesus knows no geographic or political boundary. No human nation holds a monopoly on Jesus' Kingdom. Every Christian, no matter where they live on the globe, is part of the one people of God.

Every Kingdom citizen recognizes that their primary citizenship is in heaven. Christians in the United States must be like the fathers and mothers of our faith who lived in exile with hope, knowing there will come a day when we will enter God's City. The primary document that should shape the beliefs and lifestyle of every Christian in America is not the Constitution, but God's Word. The ruler and commander in chief of our lives is not the president of the United States but King Jesus. This is not a cry for anarchy, but rather a recalibration for each of us to get our priorities straight. The Christian faith did not begin in 1492, 1620, or 1776. Ours is a faith that has withstood the test of time for over three millennia.

A HOPE-FILLED RESPONSE

When we begin to understand our Kingdom ethnicity, hope will refuel our hearts. We will unhitch our faith from the restrictions of American syncretism and discover faith that transcends culture, ethnicity, geography, and even time. We will receive constant pushback from the nonbelieving world as well as from Christians who are still choosing syncretism, but we will be able to "count it all joy" in the face of trials (James 1:2).

When you begin living out the transcendent faith Jesus calls us to, don't be surprised by pushback, persecution, or trolling on social media. Don't expect the world to embrace the Jesus you are following. Don't be caught off guard when professing Christians object to your work of ethnic conciliation. You will encounter trials as much as Los Angeles citizens experience traffic. As James assures us, God allows these trials so our faith will mature while we follow Jesus.

In James 1:3, the word *testing* comes from the idea of something being tried in order to be found true, like the process of purifying precious metals.[4] When I was growing up, my pastor, George Westlake Jr., often shared a story of a silversmith to describe why we encounter trials. A young man walked into a silversmith's shop and asked how he made the silver furnishings that were in the window. The silversmith welcomed the young man into the back of his shop and showed him a dirty, muddy, clumpy rock. Then he opened an oven that had been heating for hours. The silversmith put the dirty rock on a spoon, put the spoon in the oven, and closed the door. And they waited. When the silversmith saw the young man growing impatient, he opened the oven and pulled the spoon's long handle toward him. The rock was smaller, but the silversmith put it back into the oven and closed the door.

The young man was puzzled. "What is going on?" he asked the silversmith.

The silversmith told him that the silver was not yet ready. The process continued for the remainder of the workday. Just as the young man was ready to give up and walk out, the silversmith told him to stop and wait. The young man was flustered but complied, and the silversmith opened the oven door, pulled out the spoon, and said, "The silver is ready."

"How do you know it's ready?" the young man asked the silversmith.

"When I look in the spoon," the silversmith said, "and I'm able to see my reflection, I know that the impurities have been burned out, and all that remains is pure silver." Now the silver could be poured into the mold and used for his creations.

God allows us to endure trials because trials purge the impurities—the ways we do not reflect the Kingdom ethics of Jesus—out of us. God wants to see His reflection in our lives so He can mold us into what He wants us to be. Then we can be used by Him for His glory. James says that "the testing of [our] faith produces steadfastness" (James 1:3). As we allow God to shape us, we will continue to be molded into what He has called us to display through the local church.

God is calling His followers in America to stop fighting His process of purification. We fight His process by avoiding discomfort and conflict that can actually lead to reconciliation and purification in our interpersonal relationships within God's family. The work of ethnic conciliation calls each of us to free ourselves from cultural practices that are not in step with the Kingdom ethics we are called to live.

This purification will cause us to let go of our comforts, our addiction to entertainment, the ways we ignore the sin of partiality, and the superiority complexes that manifest themselves in the thirst for political power. We must work diligently to no longer allow the American middle-class profile to be the picture of Christianity. We must not align ourselves politically as if a political party is a gang affiliation. Kingdom ethnicity should be a priority for every believer because of our hope in the coming Kingdom of Jesus.

THE BROCHURE OF HEAVEN

Years ago, in the middle of winter in Kansas City, I received an invitation to speak at a resort in Florida. When Elicia and I googled the resort's website, we saw pictures of clear-blue water with white sand, palm trees, and bright-blue sky. The resort had amazing amenities—a fitness room, a spa, a large swimming pool. Each room was a suite with a living room, a king-size bed, and a Jacuzzi.

I looked away from the pictures of the beautiful place where we would be going in the future and out my window to the gray skies of winter in Kansas City. The snow on the ground was no longer white but brown; it was mixed with sand and mud. The air was frigid, and the people walking by were bundled up. My reality seemed so far from the future Floridian paradise.

This is our present tension. We live in a cold world. With each video that goes viral, each grievous hate-filled attack, we wonder if winter will ever end. Take heart, my dear brothers and sisters—our future is the paradise of God! The book of Revelation shows us what life in the City of God looks like—the unity and rejoicing of every ethnicity—and this should fill our hearts with hope. We must keep looking at God's Word to remind us of our hope: Jesus will make all things new (Revelation 21:5).

When I read Scripture, I long to be with Jesus in the City of God, just as looking at the resort website made me long for the warmth of Florida. Yet I had to remain where I was and work until the day of my arrival—just as God's church in America must continue His work while it is winter. The world needs to see us doing the work of ethnic conciliation. When local churches are flooded with believers who know and embrace esperanza, our hope-filled responses to the cold, hate-filled world serve as brochures of heaven for our communities! Let's serve them well.

ACKNOWLEDGMENTS

To Elicia, Izabelle, Lola, and Duce:
Thank you for supporting me by walking with me.

To Reach Fellowship:
Thank you for loving me.

APPENDIX

Acronyms

ABLE

- *Apply Wisdom* (Matthew 10:16): Be evangelistic during the time of interaction. But don't be overly romantic. Expect some hostility because the convictions of those you're alongside may not be rooted in or in pursuit of Jesus.

- *Be Clear* (2 Corinthians 6:14-18): Realize that your mission is to represent God's Kingdom and live out Kingdom ethics. Jesus' church transcends the social ills you're addressing. Remember, the gospel's power does not rise or fall because of partnership with any movement. So clearly communicate short-term participation in cobelligerency, and make sure you continue gospel-saturated work in your community after these events are over, without partnering with the cobelligerents, to safeguard your biblical convictions and the distinction of the church's mission.

- *Live Pure* (Ephesians 5:1-14): Abstain from any sinful activities that those in your cobelligerency practice. If, while joining them in lobbying or protest, you decide to participate in acts of hate, sensuality, or other forms of sin, you're no longer distinct in morality or mission and must confess (1 John 1:8-10), repent (2 Corinthians 7:9-11), and seek restoration (Galatians 6:1-2).

- *Engage Responsibly* (James 1:22-27): Be committed in ministering to the widows, orphans, and poor in your city that are part of the systemic oppression. Evangelicals in your city may have often neglected these people before, and your commitment will show cobelligerents your long-term priorities.

FABRIC

- *Family*—The Christian home is the first mission field, and those within the local church should model and multiply a Jesus-centered emphasis that mirrors Ephesians 5:22–6:4, Colossians 3:18–4:1, and 1 Peter 3:1-7. Since the church is God's family, our understanding of family should include nuance and space for blended families, unmarried believers,[1] and foster care and adoptive members. All of these voices have value; none are second-class citizens in the Kingdom.

- *Authority* (Scripture, government, and law enforcement)—We must model what it looks like to pray for our national, state, and local leaders (1 Timothy 2:1-6). Additionally, we must couple our prayers with a lifestyle of submission to the authority of God's Word first and our government authorities second (Romans 13:1-7; 1 Peter 2:13-17). Yet we must also consider the call to speak out against injustice and mobilize to do justice on both spiritual and social levels in our community.

- *Business*—We must consider how our finances will help those in need (Philippians 4:10-20) and flourish the communities we worship in. We must show store owners in our neighborhood that God's people practice generosity and contentment (1 Timothy 6:6-10). All the while, we must seek to help the unemployed find employment, even if that means creating job opportunities for them.

- *Religion*—We must ask Jesus to fill our hearts with His compassion (Matthew 9:35-38) as we reasonably respond to those who oppose our faith (1 Peter 3:13-17). We must diligently discover how to translate God's story to people groups living in our proximity and reach out to them as we make Christ known. In addition, we must offer apologetic insights to counter the ethnocentric cults that proselytize Christians of non-European descent who struggle with not having their ethnicity affirmed.

- *Institutions* (education, elder care, and rehabilitation)—We must invest time in securing employment and in volunteering in local schools, retirement homes, hospice centers, jails, and prisons. We must also lobby for education and prison reform to enter our community; we must respond to the cries of our city that resemble Psalm 10:10-18.

- *Culture* (arts and entertainment)—We must view the culture through the lens of God's story before we engage it. We must examine the culture's belief system, language, and practices in light of Scripture so we can find ways to relate while remaining morally pure. Our speech should be filled with hope and concepts the culture can understand so that we can build relationships with the people around us. We will fight against sinning to gain approval (Acts 17:16-34). The relationships we develop will be in harmony with Paul's method in 1 Thessalonians 2:8.

HUMAN

- *Habitat* (social spaces)—addressing issues working against flourishing in the home, church, community, city, nation, and world.

- *Understanding* (intellect)—learning and processing history, the present, and the projected future righteously.

- *Material* (physical bodies)—acknowledging and striving to meet dietary needs, clothing, exercise, employment opportunities, fair wages, hygiene, righteous sexual expression, and affordable housing for self and others.

- *Affection* (emotions)—developing healthy pathways of becoming aware, coping, expressing, and healing in the areas of emotions, mental illnesses, stress factors, and abuse (emotional, physical, sexual, spiritual, substance, and verbal).

- *Non-Material* (spiritual)—recognizing the God-given soul that every image bearer has received and sharing the Good News that Jesus as the only qualified Savior who redeems.

PACE

- *Patience*—God is patient with all His children, so all His children must be patient with each other. This means we must fight off passive aggressiveness and communicate honestly when we are frustrated, disappointed, or offended. Conflict is a litmus test for relationships. It shows the level of depth a relationship has. When conflict arises, if a relationship is shallow, allowing things to simmer under the surface can go on for an extended amount of time, preventing the relationship from going deeper. If the relationship is meaningful, the issue will be resolved and the relationship will grow deeper than before the conflict surfaced.

- *Active Listening*—This is a call to hear the developing leader's heart, not just their tone. If they lacked a father figure in their life, they may have a hard time trusting or committing to a discipleship relationship. If they had traumatic childhood experiences, they may struggle to maintain healthy relationships. Active listening is essential; the diamond in the rough must be given the opportunity to open up and vent about their heart wounds. This may be the first time in their life they've felt safe enough to take this risk. Do not abandon them after they have done this.

- *Correct* (when necessary)—Part of Jesus' design for discipleship includes teaching others to obey His spiritual and social commands. Teaching is not just transferring information but coming alongside and walking with another person who is being transformed by the same Holy Spirit. At times, behavior patterns and sin will need to be identified, called out, and corrected. Growth and maturity also need to be identified and affirmed. Both are crucial in developing the diamond in the rough.

- *Equip*—The gospel speaks not only to the theology of the believer but also to their whole being. Leaders must walk holistically with their potential leaders. They must share tools that deal with emotional intelligence, financial stewardship, mental health, sexual purity, soul care, and time management, to name a few. The more well-rounded a leader is, the better they can help meet the needs of their church and community.

RAPID

- *Restore* dignity to every image bearer by helping meet their HUMAN needs

- *Affirm* the ethnic identity of every Jesus follower (fellow Kingdom citizens)

- *Promote* the Kingdom ethics Jesus commands us to practice socially and spiritually

- *Institute* the work of ethnic conciliation and weave the gospel into the FABRIC of your community

- *Develop* biblical guardrails for limited engagement with nonbelievers as cobelligerents

NOTES

INTRODUCTION

1. David Daniels, "St. Louis Rapper Thi'sl Takes Action after Michael Brown Killing," *Rapzilla*, August 15, 2014, http://rapzilla.com/2014-08-st-louis -rapper-thi-sl-takes-action-after-michael-brown-killing/.

2. Siang-Yang Tan and Eric T. Scalise, *Lay Counseling: Equipping Christians for a Helping Ministry* (Grand Rapids, MI: Zondervan, 2016), 227.

3. In *The End of White Christian America*, founding CEO of the Public Religion Research Institute (PRRI) Robert P. Jones argues that white American Christianity (divided into two subgroups, mainline and evangelical) is dying. He supports his argument based on the declining numbers of white American Christian adherents, the fact that political policies are no longer subjugated to what white American Christians classify as ethical, and the generational differences in worldview that permeate our society. According to Jones, each of these components has dethroned the white American Christian voice from being the dominant leader of the conversation and the picture of what defines America.

4. Derwin L. Gray, *The High Definition Leader: Building Multiethnic Churches in a Multiethnic World* (Nashville: Thomas Nelson, 2015), 2.

5. Frank Newport, "2017 Update on Americans and Religion," *Gallup*, December 22, 2017, https://news.gallup.com/poll/224642/2017-update -americans-religion.aspx. Robert P. Jones provides the 1975 percentage of Protestantism in "The Eclipse of White Christian America," *The Atlantic*, July 12, 2016, https://www.theatlantic.com/politics/archive/2016/07 /the-eclipse-of-white-christian-america/490724/.

6. "The phrase 'Global South' refers broadly to the regions of Latin America, Asia, Africa, and Oceans. It is one of a family of terms . . . that denote regions outside Europe and North America, mostly . . . low income and often politically or culturally marginalized. . . . The term Global South functions as more than a metaphor for underdevelopment." Nour Dados and Raewyn Connell, "The Global South," *Contexts* (SAGE Journals) 11, no. 1 (February 14, 2012), 12–13, https://journals.sagepub.com/doi/pdf/10.1177/1536504212436479.

7. The given mission of the church is a compilation of the following stated convictions: DeYoung and Gilbert's emphasis on evangelism in *What Is the Mission of the Church?: Making Sense of Social Justice, Shalom, and the Great Commission* (Wheaton, IL: Crossway, 2011), Keller's focus on local churches training members to engage the culture in *Center Church: Doing Balanced, Gospel-Centered Ministry in Your City* (Grand Rapids, MI: Zondervan, 2012), and Hammett's intentional inclusion of the nations as a nonnegotiable in *Biblical Foundations for Baptist Churches: A Contemporary Ecclesiology* (Grand Rapids, MI: Kregel, 2005).

8. Because of the nuances of the political connection with the term *Hispanic*, and its inclusion within the constructed "white race," I have chosen to use the term *Latino* to reference the ethnicity of myself and others whose family roots are in Mexico, Latin America, South America, and the Caribbean. For further reading on the distinctions between Hispanic and Latino, please see *The Hispanic Condition: The Power of a People* by Ilan Stavans, *Harvest of Empire: A History of Latinos in America* by Juan Gonzalez, and *American Nations: A History of the Eleven Rival Regional Cultures of North America* by Colin Woodard.

9. I view ethnicity and culture as two different elements. Ethnicity identifies the heritage of our family descent, while culture is something developed by normal life rhythms. Culture involves beliefs, language, and social structures. It is possible for people to have the same ethnicity yet be shaped differently based on the culture they were raised in.

10. When I use the masculine term *Latino(s)* in the general sense, I do so not to exclude women but merely to avoid awkward constructions like *Latina/o, Latin@,* or *Latinx*. Generic references to *Latino(s)*, therefore, implicitly include *Latina(s)*.

11. David G. Gutiérrez, "An Historic Overview of Latino Immigration and the Demographic Transformation of the United States," National Park Service, U.S. Department of the Interior, accessed January 30, 2017, https://www.nps.gov/heritageinitiatives/latino/latinothemestudy/immigration.htm.

12. Antonio Flores, "Facts on U.S. Latinos, 2015," Pew Research Center, http://www.pewhispanic.org/2017/09/18/facts-on-u-s-latinos/.

13. Jens Manuel Krogstad, "Key Facts About How the U.S. Hispanic Population Is Changing," Pew Research Center, September 8, 2016, http://www.pewresearch.org/fact-tank/2016/09/08/key-facts-about-how -the-u-s-hispanic-population-is-changing/.

14. Influencers in the areas of politics, economics, and education not only noticed the burgeoning Latino demographic but also focused on winning their affections. Politically speaking, conservatives desired a similar cultural assimilation as the eastern and southern European immigrants of old (see David R. Roediger's *Working Toward Whiteness: How America's Immigrants Became White*). Latinos were shrewdly classified as *Hispanics*, falsely promoting them as a heterogeneous group, part of the socially constructed "white race" (Ilan Stavans, *The Hispanic Condition: The Power of a People*, New York: Harper Collins, 2001, 23–24). It wasn't until recent years, when conservatives saw that their efforts were only bearing fruit among Cubans (as read in Juan Gonzalez's *Harvest of Empire: A History of Latinos in America*), that they shifted their thinking and began working with diligence to woo other Latinos away from the Democratic Party, which has maintained the Latino voting bloc en masse since the late 1960s (Colin Woodard, *American Nations: A History of the Eleven Rival Regional Cultures of North America*; New York: Penguin, 2011, 32–33).

15. In the world of economics, the surge of the Latino population has affected American housing-market trends, labor-market opportunities, and wages earned. Sections IV and V of David L. Leal and Stephen J. Trejo's *Latinos and the Economy: Integration and Impact in Schools, Labor Markets, and Beyond* (New York: Springer Press, 2011) provide comprehensive research on native and immigrant Hispanics and their earnings, effect on minimum wage, and labor skills, in addition to how all of this has affected housing prices in the United States. The massive amount of disposable income within the Latino population ($1.1 trillion annual spending power) has turned the heads of advertising and marketing executives. If this demographic were an autonomous country, it would rank sixteenth in the global market (Joe Uva in David Rennie's "America's Hispanics: From Minor to Major," *The Economist*, March 12, 2015, http://www.economist. com/news/special-report/21645996-one-american-six-now-hispanic-up -small-minority-two-generations-ago).

16. In the United States, 17.9 million Latinos (one third of the Latino population) are under the age of 18, and 14.6 million of US Latinos are Millennials (ages 18 to 33 in the year 2014; Eileen Patten, "The Nation's Latino Population Is Defined by Its Youth," Pew Research, April 20, 2016, http://www.pewhispanic.org/2016/04/20/the-nations-latino -population-is-defined-by-its-youth/). As Carlos Ortiz reported in the

Journal of Hispanic Higher Education, "the Hispanic population has grown at a rapid rate and yet has remained the lowest-achieving group in education." (Carlos J. Ortiz, Melissa A. Valerio, and Kristina Lopez, "Trends in Hispanic Academic Achievement: Where Do We Go from Here?," *Journal of Hispanic Higher Education* 11, no. 2 [April 2012]: 137). Higher education institutions have noticed and are successfully marketing to the Latino population, resulting in a significant Latino college-enrollment increase (Jens Manuel Krogstad, "5 Facts about Latinos and Education," Pew Research, July 28, 2016, http://www.pewresearch.org /fact-tank/2016/07/28/5-facts-about-latinos-and-education/). Schools are beginning to recruit in areas where the Latino population is dense, no matter their geographic distance. The University of New Hampshire understands that recruitment of Latino students begins during their early years of education, and sponsoring programs such as Upward Bound have proven successful in helping Latino students transition from high school to college (Kimberly Greenwood, "Higher Education Marketing to the Hispanic Student Population," honors theses, University of New Hampshire, 2012, http://scholars.unh.edu/cgi/viewcontent.cgi?article =1049&context=honors).

17. Cary Funk and Jessica Hamar Martinez, "The Shifting Religious Identity of Latinos in the Unites States: Nearly One-in-Four Latinos Are Former Catholics," Pew Research, May 7, 2014, http://www.pewforum.org/2014 /05/07/the-shifting-religious-identity-of-latinos-in-the-united-states/. Jessica Martínez and Michael Lipka, "Hispanic Millennials Are Less Religious than Older U.S. Hispanics," Pew Research, May 8, 2014, http://www.pewresearch.org/fact-tank/2014/05/08/hispanic-millennials -are-less-religious-than-older-u-s-hispanics/.

18. I'm in a position of privilege to be able to write on ethnic conciliation, but if you look at all my endnotes, I reference men and women from various ethnicities whose work I'm learning from.

19. Alvin L. Schutmaat wrote "Canto de Esperanza (Song of Hope)" out of his work in Latin America and set it to an Argentine folk melody. For full lyrics and history, see Diana Sanchez-Bushong, "History of Hymns: "Canto de Esperanza (Song of Hope)," Discipleship Ministries, accessed March 19, 2019, https://www.umcdiscipleship.org/resources/history-of -hymns-canto-de-esperanza-song-of-hope.

CHAPTER 1: WHAT IS ETHNIC CONCILIATION?

1. I want to be clear up front that just because I believe there is only one race, the human race, that does not mean that I am endorsing what I call Christian color blindness (a term I will unpack in chapter 5).

2. Thomas L. Constable, "Notes on Acts: 2017 Edition," PDF version, 243, https://planobiblechapel.org/tcon/notes/pdf/acts.pdf.

3. Jarvis J. Williams and Kevin M. Jones, *Removing the Stain of Racism from the Southern Baptist Convention: Diverse African American and White Perspectives* (Nashville: B&H Academic, 2017), 27.

4. Anibal Quijano, "Coloniality of Power, Eurocentrism, and Latin America," *Nepantla: Views from the South* 1, no. 3 (2000): 534, https://www.decolonialtranslation.com/english/quijano-coloniality-of-power.pdf.

5. Quijano, "Coloniality of Power," 575.

6. I have tried to set a pathway forward regarding affirming ethnicities by removing "color-coded" language from my text. I will honor the work of others who use it in quotes I cite from them. As for me, for the most part, I have replaced the term *white* with *of European descent* and *black* with *African American*. I do use the term *brown* to reference my personal voice, one that I am still developing. My intention in doing this is because ethnicity and culture are two distinct realities. Since brown is the color that surfaces when all primary colors intersect, I call myself brown because of cultural and ethnic realities.

7. Robert Con Davis-Undiano, *Mestizos Come Home!: Making and Claiming Mexican American Identity* (Norman, OK: University of Oklahoma, 2017), 36.

8. Roberta Estes, "Las Castas—Spanish Racial Classifications," Native Heritage Project, June 15, 2013, https://nativeheritageproject.com/2013/06/15/las-castas-spanish-racial-classifications/.

9. Ilona Katzew, *Casta Painting: Images of Race in Eighteenth-Century Mexico* (New Haven, CT: Yale University, 2005), 40.

10. YouTube, "John Sayles Reads Bartolome de Las Casas," January 27, 2008, https://www.youtube.com/watch?v=9qOnq4qQKAw. To read about Montesinos standing up for indigenous people's rights, see https://www.pbs.org/conquistadors/devaca/lascasas_01.html.

11. Rodolfo F. Acuña, *Occupied America: A History of Chicanos*, 7th ed. (Upper Saddle River, NJ: Pearson, 2011), 21.

12. Mark Charles, "Regarding the Term 'Merciless Indian Savages,'" Wirelesshogan (blog), July 4, 2018, https://wirelesshogan.blogspot.com/2018/07/regarding-term-merciless-indian-savages.html.

13. Mark Charles, "The Doctrine of Discovery: A Lecture by Mark Charles in Fresno CA," YouTube, May 27, 2018, https://youtu.be/XRRDuInkgrI?t=48m16s.

14. Donald M. Scott, "The Religious Origins of Manifest Destiny," National Humanities Center, accessed March 20, 2019, http://nationalhumanitiescenter.org/tserve/nineteen/nkeyinfo/mandestiny.htm.

15. John C. Pinheiro, *Missionaries of Republicanism: A Religious History of the Mexican-American War* (Oxford, UK: Oxford University Press, 2014).

16. Martha Menchaca, *Recovering History, Constructing Race: The Indian, Black, and White Roots of Mexican Americans* (Austin, TX: University of Texas Press, 2001), 12.

17. For further reading, please consider *The Color of Compromise: The Truth about the American Church's Complicity in Racism* by Jemar Tisby and the forthcoming *Truth Be Told* by Mark Charles and Soong-Chan Rah.

18. Richard S. Newman, *Freedom's Prophet: Bishop Richard Allen, the AME Church, and the Black Founding Fathers* (New York: New York University Press, 2008).

CHAPTER 2: OUR REDEMPTIVE ETHIC

1. My dear friend and author Bruce Ashford helped shape the way I communicate God's story.

2. Walter A. Elwell and Barry J. Beitzel, *Baker Encyclopedia of the Bible*, vol. 1 (Grand Rapids, MI: Baker Book House, 1988), 1017.

3. For more on this cultural mandate, see Subby Szterszky, "The Cultural Mandate: Living as Divine Imager-Bearers," Focus on the Family Canada, accessed April 10, 2019, https://www.focusonthefamily.ca/content/the -cultural-mandate-living-as-divine-image-bearers.

4. Alan Cairns, *Dictionary of Theological Terms*, exp. 3rd ed. (Greenville, SC: Ambassador Emerald International, 2002), 121.

5. Walter A. Elwell, *Baker Encyclopedia of the Bible*, vol. 2 (Grand Rapids, MI: Baker Book House, 1988), 1967.

6. William G. T. Shedd, *Dogmatic Theology*, 3rd ed., Alan W. Gomes, ed. (Phillipsburg, NJ: P&R, 2003), 956.

7. *Merriam-Webster*, s.v. "impute (v.)," accessed April 10, 2019, https://www .merriam-webster.com/dictionary/impute.

CHAPTER 3: OTRA VEZ

1. I am aware the word *conciled* is currently not in the dictionary; however, I am compelled to use it, for two reasons. First, *conciled* describes the state of humanity's relationship with God pre-Fall. Second, Ian Woodley kindly explains the beauty of using the word *conciled* to understand *reconciled* ("Are You Conciled?," Nottingham Grace Communion, April 24, 2015, https://nottingham.gcichurches.org/2015/04/are-you-conciled/).

2. I. Howard Marshall, *The Gospel of Luke: A Commentary on the Greek Text*, New International Greek Testament Commentary (Grand Rapids, MI: Paternoster, 1978), 449.

3. Robert H. Stein, The New American Commentary, vol. 24, *Luke* (Nashville: B&H, 1992), 318.

4. The verb translated "saw" is written in the contemporaneous participle, which means that Jesus looked at the people during the same time he acted with compassion (Albert L. Lukaszewski, *The Lexham Syntactic Greek New Testament Glossary* [Lexham Press, 2007]). According to Barclay, the verb that expresses Jesus' empathy here "describes the compassion which moves a man to the deepest depths of his being" (quoted in David Guzik, "Study Guide for Matthew 9," accessed April 10, 2019, https://www .blueletterbible.org/Comm/guzik_david/StudyGuide_Mat/Mat_9.cfm).

5. For dealing with more complex, nuanced, or even public sins, a good primer to consider is *Restoring Those Who Fall: A Church Discipline Statement* by Jim Elliff and Daryl Wingerd.

6. Robert Jamieson, A. R. Fausset, and David Brown, *A Commentary, Critical and Explanatory, on the Old and New Testaments*, vol. 2 (Hartford, CT: S. S. Scranton, 1871), 109. In this commentary, the term *Samaritan* is said to be synonymous with *heretic* and *devil*; it was culturally understood by Jews as a degrading term when someone of Jewish ethnicity used it.

7. Biblical Studies Press, *The NET Bible First Edition Notes* (Spokane, WA: Biblical Studies Press, 2006).

CHAPTER 4: THE SIN OF PARTIALITY

1. Eugene H. Merrill, The New American Commentary, vol. 4, *Deuteronomy* (Nashville: Broadman & Holman, 1994), 204.

2. William Barclay, *The Letters of James and Peter*, Daily Study Bible Series, 2nd ed. (Edinburgh: Saint Andrew, 1964), 76.

3. See Lexicon in "Matthew 7:12," BibleHub, accessed April 10, 2019, https://biblehub.com/lexicon/matthew/7-12.htm.

4. Diane Langberg, *Suffering and the Heart of God: How Trauma Destroys and Christ Restores* (Greensboro, NC: New Growth, 2015), 8.

5. John B. Polhill, The New American Commentary, vol. 26, *Acts* (Nashville: Broadman & Holman, 1992), 179.

6. Thomas L. Constable, "Notes on Galatians: 2019 Edition," accessed March 26, 2019, 39, https://planobiblechapel.org/tcon/notes/pdf/galatians.pdf.

CHAPTER 5: COLOR-BLIND CHRISTIANITY

1. Jon Acuff, who coined this phrase, describes it as follows: "The Jesus Juke is when someone takes what is clearly a joke filled conversation and completely reverses direction into something serious and holy" ("The Jesus Juke," *Stuff Christians Like*, November 16, 2010, http://stuffchristianslike .net/2010/11/16/the-jesus-juke/).

2. Legacy Disciple, "Lecrae, Soong-Chan Rah, Elicia Horton & Joe Thorn: The People of God and Diversity," December 24, 2015, https://www .youtube.com/watch?v=nolvRhq6NRQ.

3. Rich Tatum, "How to Treat One Another," *Christianity Today*, July 12, 2011, https://www.christianitytoday.com/biblestudies/articles/bibleinsights /how-to-treat-one-another.html.

4. To learn more, I suggest reading Joseph H. Hellerman's *When the Church Was a Family: Recapturing Jesus' Vision for Authentic Christian Community* (Nashville: B & H, 2009).

CHAPTER 6: TANGIBLE REPENTANCE

1. Jim Wallis, *America's Original Sin: Racism, White Privilege, and the Bridge to a New America* (Grand Rapids, MI: Brazos, 2016), 9.

2. "What Is Pneumonia and Why Can It Be So Deadly?," BBC, April 19, 2013, http://www.bbc.co.uk/science/0/21969416.

3. Thomas L. Constable, "Notes on Numbers: 2019 Edition," accessed March 26, 2019, 27, http://planobiblechapel.org/tcon/notes/pdf/numbers.pdf.

4. My friend Adam Thomason offers commentary on these truths in his book *Confessions of an Ex-Evangelical: Why I Left Christianity and Started Practicing Jesus*, which is accessible for free here: http://www.iamredrev .com/new-book.

5. Rachel L. Swarns, "272 Slaves Were Sold to Save Georgetown. What Does It Owe Their Descendants?," *New York Times*, April 16, 2016, https:// www.nytimes.com/2016/04/17/us/georgetown-university-search-for -slave-descendants.html.

6. Swarns, "272 Slaves Were Sold."

7. Rachel L. Swarns, "Georgetown University Plans Steps to Atone for Slave Past," *New York Times*, September 1, 2016, https://www.nytimes.com /2016/09/02/us/slaves-georgetown-university.html.

8. Susan Svrluga, "'Make it Right': Descendants of Slaves Demand Restitution from Georgetown," *Washington Post*, January 17, 2018, https://www.washingtonpost.com/news/grade-point/wp/2018/01/16 /__trashed-2/?utm_term=.239523f93848.

9. BibleHub, "1189. deomai," accessed April 10, 2019, https://biblehub .com/greek/1189.htm.

10. Michelle Higgins, Christina Edmondson, and Ekemini Uwan host the podcast *Truth's Table*, which has released a four-part series titled "Reparations NOW" (https://soundcloud.com/truthstable).

CHAPTER 7: HOW SHOULD THE CHURCH RESPOND?

1. In a book I wrote with my wife, *Enter the Ring: Fighting Together for a Gospel-Saturated Marriage*, we consider the single, divorced, single parents, and widowed nuances in our term for *unmarried*. Our appendix helps churches affirm and empower these saints so they aren't marginalized in church life or discussions about family.

2. This list summarizes six issues listed by Christopher Brooks in his book *Urban Apologetics: Why the Gospel Is Good News for the City* (Grand Rapids, MI: Kregel, 2014).

3. *The Complete Works of Francis A. Schaeffer*, vol. 4, *A Christian View of the Church*, 2nd ed. (Wheaton, IL: Crossway, 1985), 30–31.

4. Martin Wroe and Dave Roberts, "Dr Francis Schaeffer," in *Adrift in the 80's: The Strait Interviews*, ed. and comp. Stewart Henderson (Basingstoke, UK: Marshall Morgan and Scott, 1986), 31.

5. "America's Urban Population: Patterns & Characteristics," ProximityOne, accessed March 28. 2019, http://proximityone.com/urbanpopulation.htm.

6. William H. Frey, "The Browning of America," Milken Institute Review, October 19, 2015, http://www.milkenreview.org/articles/charticle-3.

7. Dennis Cauchon and Paul Overberg, "Census Data Shows Minorities Now a Majority of U.S. Births," *USA Today*, updated May 17, 2012, http://usatoday30.usatoday.com/news/nation/story/2012-05-17/minority-births-census/55029100/1.

8. Ray Oldenburg, *The Great Good Place: Cafés, Coffee Shops, Bookstores, Bars, Hair Salons and Other Hangouts at the Heart of a Community* (Cambridge, MA: Da Capo, 1999), 16.

9. For further reading on this topic, please see *Aliens in the Promised Land: Why Minority Leadership Is Overlooked in White Christian Churches and Institutions*, edited by Anthony B. Bradley.

CHAPTER 8: KINGDOM ETHICS FOR A KINGDOM ETHNICITY

1. Francis A. Schaeffer, *A Christian Manifesto* (Wheaton, IL: Crossway, 2005), 121.

2. For example, see pastor and author John MacArthur's discussion on the gospel and race for Christian Defense International (Christian Defense International, "The Gospel and Black Lives Matter" YouTube video, 04:5, posted July 13, 2018, https://www.youtube.com/watch?v=pkOv94cyfc4). In the video, the moderator frames the question by identifying the shooting of Mike Brown in Ferguson, Missouri, alongside the Black Lives Matter movement, then asks MacArthur how a pastor who is not leading a predominantly African American congregation should address the current issues while refraining from being known as a "social-justice

church." MacArthur responds by placing the gospel message in a separate category from the stated racial issues in question (leveraging Galatians 3:28 as proof for doing so), and says such things are "a nonissue" before sharing his personal engagement in the civil rights movement in the 1960s to frame his concluding thought: "When the gospel changes your life, you go from social issues to spiritual issues."

3. For example, in his book *Democracy Matters: Winning the Fight against Imperialism*, Dr. Cornel West says that "To be a Christian—a follower of Jesus Christ—is to love wisdom, love justice, and love freedom. This is the radical love in Christian freedom and the radical freedom in Christian love that embraces Socratic questioning, prophetic witness, and tragicomic hope" (New York: Penguin, 2004; page 172). West presents Christianity as a faith not of seeking Jesus for forgiveness of sins or embracing his shed blood as the atonement necessary to remove sin debt but instead as striving to embody wisdom, justice, and freedom.

Here's the tension I live in: I was educated and trained by those in the former, but I live and minister among those of the latter. I navigate this tension by drinking deeply from wells of wisdom: namely, C. René Padilla, Samuel Escobar, and Orlando Costas, developers of Misión Integral (which is, in my opinion, the most balanced method of dissolving this tension). Misión Integral was developed in Latin America during a time of economic, political, and theological upheaval. C. René Padilla coined the phrase *misión integral* during his plenary speech at the 1974 Lausanne Congress (C. René Padilla, "Holistic Mission," Lausanne Occasional Paper 33, September 29, 2004, https://www.lausanne.org/content/holistic-mission-lop-33#hm).

4. BibleHub, "1383. dokimion," accessed April 11, 2019, https://biblehub.com/greek/1383.htm.

APPENDIX: ACRONYMS

1. In a book I wrote with my wife, *Enter the Ring: Fighting Together for a Gospel-Saturated Marriage*, we consider the single, divorced, single parents, and widowed nuances in our term for *unmarried*. Our appendix helps churches affirm and empower these saints so they aren't marginalized in church life or discussions about family.

FIGHT *for your* MARRIAGE

You can have a thriving and vibrant marriage.

Through the vulnerable lens of their own struggles, D. A. and Elicia Horton bring a powerful and original approach to important marital issues such as communication, money, spiritual life, and sexual intimacy. Living out the gospel in your marriage will equip you to face whatever comes.

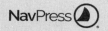

THE NAVIGATORS® STORY

T HANK YOU for picking up this NavPress book! I hope it has been a blessing to you.

NavPress is a ministry of The Navigators. The Navigators began in the 1930s, when a young California lumberyard worker named Dawson Trotman was impacted by basic discipleship principles and felt called to teach those principles to others. He saw this mission as an echo of 2 Timothy 2:2: "And the things you have heard me say in the presence of many witnesses entrust to reliable people who will also be qualified to teach others" (NIV).

In 1933, Trotman and his friends began discipling members of the US Navy. By the end of World War II, thousands of men on ships and bases around the world were learning the principles of spiritual multiplication by the intentional, person-to-person teaching of God's Word.

After World War II, The Navigators expanded its relational ministry to include college campuses; local churches; the Glen Eyrie Conference Center and Eagle Lake Camps in Colorado Springs, Colorado; and neighborhood and citywide initiatives across the country and around the world.

Today, with more than 2,600 US staff members—and local ministries in more than 100 countries—The Navigators continues the transformational process of making disciples who make more disciples, advancing the Kingdom of God in a world that desperately needs the hope and salvation of Jesus Christ and the encouragement to grow deeper in relationship with Him.

NAVPRESS was created in 1975 to advance the calling of The Navigators by bringing biblically rooted and culturally relevant products to people who want to know and love Christ more deeply. In January 2014, NavPress entered an alliance with Tyndale House Publishers to strengthen and better position our rich content for the future. Through *THE MESSAGE* Bible and other resources, NavPress seeks to bring positive spiritual movement to people's lives.

If you're interested in learning more or becoming involved with The Navigators, go to www.navigators.org. For more discipleship content from The Navigators and NavPress authors, visit www.thedisciplemaker.org. May God bless you in your walk with Him!

Sincerely,

DON PAPE
VP/PUBLISHER, NAVPRESS

www.navpress.com